Exploring God

Without Getting Religious

BRUCE ROBERTS DREISBACH

Belleville, Ontario, Canada

Exploring God Without Getting Religious
Copyright © 2002, Bruce Roberts Dreisbach

All Rights Reserved. No part of this publication may be reproduced, stored in a retrieval system or transmitted in any form or by any means—electronic, mechanical, photocopy, recording or any other—except for brief quotations in printed reviews, without the prior permission of the author.

All Scripture quotations, unless otherwise specified, are from *The Holy Bible, New International Version*. Copyright © 1973, 1978, 1984 International Bible Society. Used by permission of Zondervan Publishing House. All rights reserved.

Scripture taken from *The Message*, copyright © by Eugene H. Peterson, 1993, 1994, 1995. Used by permission of NavPress Publishing Group.

Scriptures identified as NCV are quoted from *The Holy Bible, New Century Version* copyright © 1987, 1988, 1991 by Word Publishing, Nashville, Tennessee. Used by permission.

"One of Us," written by Eric Bazilian, copyright © 1995 PolyGram Records, Inc. ASCAP. All rights reserved.Used by permission.

"In the Light" by Charlie Peacock and Toby McKeehan, copyright © 1991 Sparrow Song/Audi Beat Goes On. Admin. by BMI Christian Music Publishing. All rights reserved. Used by permission.

C.S. Lewis, *Mere Christianity,* 1943, courtesy of Macmillan Publishing.

Cover design done by Jennifer Nelson—jennifer@eyeray.com

ISBN: 1-55306-369-4

First Printing, March 2002
Second Printing, December 2002

**For more information or
to order additional copies, please contact:**
New Life Center
P.O. Box 712
Wolfeboro, NH 03894 U.S.A.
Visit our Web site at: www.exploringgod.com
Toll free order #: (866) 216-5433

Guardian Books is an imprint of *Essence Publishing*, a Christian Book Publisher dedicated to furthering the work of Christ through the written word. For more information, contact:
44 Moira Street West, Belleville, Ontario, Canada K8P 1S3.
Phone: 1-800-238-6376. Fax: (613) 962-3055.
E-mail: info@essencegroup.com
Internet: www.essencegroup.com

Exploring God
Without Getting Religious

To Stewart and Mary,
good friends who gave me the motivation
to write this book.

Table of Contents

Acknowledgements 9
Introduction 11

SECTION ONE: CAN'T FIND MY WAY HOME

   1. The "Wake-Up Call" 16

   2. Seeking Home. 24

   3. Growing Up Lost. 32

   4. The Yellow Brick Road. 46

   5. Relationships. 60

   6. Life Is Difficult 67

   7. Turning Points. 73

   8. What About Religion? 81

   9. A Relationship Without Religion 91

SECTION TWO: MAKING REAL SPIRITUAL CONNECTIONS

10. God With Us.. 104
11. I'm a Mess, You're a Mess, But It's Okay........... 114
12. Two Ways to Heaven................................. 121

SECTION THREE: EXPLORING THE LIGHT

13. The Good News 130
14. Walking in the Light 135
15. Questions and Doubts 144
16. Talking With God................................... 164
17. Learning From God.................................. 173
18. No Longer Alone.................................... 180
19. A Future and a Hope................................ 190

Notes 202

Acknowledgements

I was reminded by a dear friend and early reader of this book, that I started writing this book in 1968. Like the unfolding of my life, this book has grown through the contributions of many people over the years. I don't know where to begin with thanks, there are so many who have encouraged me on the path that led to this volume.

The love and encouragement of my family, Martie, Katybeth, and Megan, provided the nurturing environment that allowed *Exploring God* to come to pass.

The leadership team and supporters of the New Life ministry also played a major role in supporting this effort. Thanks to all of you.

I owe a debt of gratitude to Carol, for your faithful, calm, and steady efforts to transform my thoughts into something others could use. Many others contributed to the creation, design, and shaping of the final product: Stu, Jennifer, Frank, Beth, Marilyn, Mary Beth, Rachael, Mindy, Jim, David, and many others—I couldn't have done it without your help.

All of the stories in this book are true. These personal stories are deeply revealing, they share profound tragedies, and they reflect radical life transformation. Many are a matter of public record; others were shared that you might see God at work in everyday life. In some cases, the names and a few details have been changed slightly to protect the privacy of those involved.

Introduction

What Do You Mean, "Exploring God?"

Rural New Hampshire is dark at night. The nearest town is four miles from my farm. With a year-round population of less than 5,000, it has few street lights, no full traffic lights, and only a couple of yellow blinkers for the whole town. When you get out to my farm and pull in the driveway, it is usually pitch black.

Most nights I get out of my truck, grab my stuff, and hustle into the house. *Burr, it's cold outside.* Even in summer, when the sun drops below the hills, the temperature plummets. Summer evenings drop to the '50s and '40s. And in winter it's 20 or 30 degrees below.

Every once in a while, for some reason I can't explain, in spite of the chill, I stop and look up. The sight unfolded in the sky above takes my breath away. The deep black velvet sky looks like a jeweler's cloth, sprinkled with hundreds of brilliant diamonds. No, *thousands* of sparkling constellations spread across the sky. No, *millions* of awe-inspiring works of art hang in the sky above. Bright ones, near ones, far ones, clusters, formations, complex geodesic shapes, even whole swaths of stars sweep across my view. The longer I look, the more I see. There must be billions!

I am awestruck. I am transfixed. In spite of the cold air, all I want to do is gaze in wonder at my discovery.

Then it hits me. This has been out here every night. *Why haven't I seen it before?* Night after night, for who knows how many years, it's been there, but I haven't noticed it. Perhaps I never bothered to look up. It's been there all along, but suddenly I'm aware of it. After tonight, my life will never be the same.

Exploring God is like that. We can easily go through life and miss some of the most obvious things about him. We start off with high hopes and expectations. We have such a clear sense of where we want to go and how to get there. Then life happens.

Best-laid plans can be derailed by a tragic accident or an unforeseen illness. Our chosen career plateaus, or worse, turn into a dead end. Some are bitterly disappointed or betrayed in close personal relationships. Others find they achieve a large measure of accomplishment or success, but when they climb to the top of the ladder, they find it is leaning on the wrong building. Even with a wonderful mate, a healthy family, a degree of success, we wake up to a nagging sense we have *missed* something very important in life. Like my experience with the night sky, something causes us to pause and ask ourselves, *Is there something more to life? Is there a spiritual dimension that will enable me to get where I want to go?*

Most adults periodically consider spiritual issues. Some of us grew up with a sense that there *is* a God who cares for us, but as we matured, we lost touch with that feeling of a caring, spiritual being. Most of us believe in God or a "higher being," but we have no idea how to connect with God in any relevant way in our personal lives.

Here's the rub. In spite of this desire for something more, many of us have also had negative encounters with religious

Introduction

institutions or people. We've been disappointed or hurt by our experience with a church, people in a church, or with people who claimed to represent God but seemed to characterize some of the worst attributes of the human race.

Can you explore God without experiencing all the negatives that have turned you off to religion? Yes! I wrote this book to discuss how you can enjoy the benefits of a strong, growing spiritual life without the negative impacts of religious behavior and thinking. Let me share my own experience and that of others who have found a way to have a relationship with God without getting religious. Read with an open mind. Consider that there may be spiritual resources all around you, but you've never noticed them or taken the time to stop and look up.

If you seek God, he will find you.

Section One

CAN'T FIND MY WAY HOME

I'm wasted and I can't find my way home.

~Steve Winwood

CHAPTER ONE

THE "WAKE-UP CALL"

Is this all there is to life? The question surged through my heart and mind as I considered my situation. I was trapped in the airport Hilton Hotel at Chicago's O'Hare Airport. Also trapped in the lap of luxury, I'll admit that—a suite of well-appointed rooms on a floor overlooking one of the centers of commercial power in the United States—but trapped nonetheless in a way of life, in a circle of "success" that just seemed to be spiraling out of control and leading me to... well, exactly *where* it was leading me to was not clear at that moment. I had a sneaking suspicion that if I came to my senses for even a few moments, and got a clear picture of where my life was headed, it would not be a place I would choose to go.

This trip, which was to change my life, had started out like many others. I was a thirty-five-year-old executive enjoying a pinnacle of success. As the Director of Marketing Research for M&M/Mars, I knew all the power and prestige that accompanied one of the top positions in my field: enormous and powerful brands to work with, major league marketplace clout, almost unlimited financial and technical resources to create innovative, high-impact business development programs—you name it.

The "Wake-Up Call"

I loved working for one of the largest and most profitable private employers in the world. Mars has a unique corporate culture, which showed my talents in their best light. I regularly received opportunities to speak to colleagues in professional settings, travel the world, and I also gained satisfaction from the challenge of transferring our corporate success to other Mars units around the world. My family enjoyed the healthy six-figure income that came with my job as well. My wife Martie, and my two lovely daughters and I lived on a gentleman's farm in the beautiful Pennsylvania countryside in northern Bucks County.

Of course, there were downsides to my "success," most notably the long hours, the long commute, and the incessant travel. I hated when *Daylight Savings Time* ended each October. It meant for the next six months I would leave home for work in the dark, drive home in the dark, and rarely catch a glimpse of sunlight during my long workdays. Each workday was usually a minimum of ten to twelve hours, but more often fifteen to eighteen hours. And then there was travelling on top of of that....

Yes, the week of my "wake-up call" began like so many others. After my too short day and a half-weekend leave with my family to decompress from a life lived on adrenaline (and to try to touch base with "normal" living), it was Sunday afternoon—time to pack for another week of business trips.

A cold February rain fell that afternoon as I left the farm under brooding gray clouds. The weather was a perfect accompaniment to my depression as I headed to the airport. Even before I got there, the sky began to spit rain and snow, icing my windshield.

After getting to the airport, I trudged through the terrible weather, walking from long-term parking to the airline terminal. My shoes and socks were soaked through. As I sat during the interminable but predictable wait for my plane, the bone-chilling cold crawled up my legs and seeped into my heart and soul.

First a delay, then a cancellation. A change to another flight, then a gate change. Time stretched on as the afternoon faded; the dinner hour passed and finally, just before 11 P.M., I took off from Newark, headed west. I felt at least a small sense of relief knowing I was headed to a professional conference in Palm Desert. If I should ever arrive, at least the weather ought to be somewhat better in Southern California.

I never did find out what February is like in Palm Desert. Later that night my flight landed in Chicago, while my luggage promptly went to Palm Desert on an earlier flight. My connecting flight never left the ground. At 3 A.M. I checked into the airport Hilton along with a small group of other business refugees. Wet, cold, and exhausted, and miserable in heart, mind, body, and soul, I fell into bed and slept. Waking in a strange hotel room, I got up to face the task of trying to salvage my trip. I pulled on the dirty, damp set of clothes I had been wearing for the past day.

I began the ordeal of working the telephone and trying to get a new flight to California. Waiting on hold, being used and abused, I flipped through the hotel promotion booklet describing the Hilton properties around the world. Beautiful four-color pictures of splendid resorts beckoned. Beaches, pools, and lots of other amenities highlighted the grim contours of my current experience as a successful, high-flying businessman.

But suddenly, right in front of that telephone, it was as if someone had put the brakes on in my life. I skidded to a complete halt. My mind seemed to be playing the "compare and contrast" exercise, mulling over my present situation, the past twenty-four hours, even the past few years. *What if my life wasn't 'the good life'?* It didn't take too long to recognize there was clear evidence my "success" had shades of Dante's Inferno infused throughout it. Frankly, the thought that I had reached the top of the ladder, but that maybe I was leaning against the *wrong* building, stunned me.

The "Wake-Up Call"

But the evidence was too strong, too real to ignore. I hung up on the airlines and I went back to the Hilton resort guide. Paging through it, I found a quiet little resort right on the beach on Sanibel Island off the coast of Florida. Picking up the phone, I got a room for the balance of the week. Then I called United Airlines and reserved the first direct flight to Florida. "Send my luggage to Sanibel Island!"

The office was next—I told them to cancel me out of the conference and put me down for vacation for the rest of the week. "I'll be back in on Monday." I called my wife to let her know about my change of plans. Within a few hours, I was in a rental car crossing the bridge from the mainland to the quiet tropical paradise of the Sanibel Island.

The balance of the week was spent resting and walking on the beach. I enjoyed sitting around in a Jimmy Buffet T-shirt and surfer shorts, just soaking in the sun and thinking. I journaled my thoughts, and I talked to my wife on the phone. I reflected on my goals, values, and hopes for life. I found that the things I believed were really important to me as a person, didn't seem to have much of an influence on my present way of life. You could even conclude that my success and lifestyle as a busy corporate executive was a complete contradiction of who I wanted to be and what I hoped my life would stand for.

Looking honestly at the people around me and ahead of me on the corporate track of success, I didn't get feelings of "can't wait to get there." Most of the guys in my firm in their forties were division presidents and made big money. But, by and large, they had lost their marriages, their children, their hair, and their health. They were isolated, lonely people who only had a life-consuming job paying them a lot of money. They had lost their moorings in life and traded it all for a form of "success." *Did I want to end up like them in ten years?* I didn't think so.

My boss, who made in excess of $750,000 a year, used to say, "People are envious of my income, but they should see my bills!" By that he meant, the alimony payments, child support, two mortgages, the ski chalet in Vail, and so on. In reality, he was a lonely guy who had a lot of income and a lot of expenses, but not much to show for it after all those years of "success." Raking it in and flushing it all down the drain—What's left when you're done?—Not a helluva lot!

My experience of a "wake-up call" is not unusual. Many of you may have had a similar experience. Often people wake up and discover their lives are not turning out as precisely as they had planned. Sometimes this is called a "mid-life crisis." Others label it "hitting the wall." Some experience it simply as a nagging feeling that they are missing out on something important in their lives.

For me, success was like a drug. When I "came to" and saw where success was leading me, I had my "wake-up call." When I was no longer "under the influence" and I "sobered up," I was really shocked by what I saw. This experience can spring from a variety of causes and can happen at different ages and stages in a person's life.

Jennifer Dickson was twenty-eight years old, and a successful buyer for a national bookstore chain. Living in Boston with her husband Tim of four years, in many ways she was the model of the successful young career woman, and an unlikely candidate for a spiritual awakening. Jennifer was raised in a wealthy family, but her parents divorced when she was in high school. She had no religious experience, but was sent to a private boarding school where she absorbed most of the values of America's upper crust. She and Tim met at the college they both attended in the upper Midwest. After school was finished, they lived together for several years; and when they married, Jennifer and Tim moved to Boston where both had successful careers in the marketplace. At

The "Wake-Up Call"

the time they arrived in Boston, neither had ever been to church nor read the Bible.

Then Jennifer discovered she was pregnant. She and Tim were delighted, but as the pregnancy progressed, things took a turn for the worst. Complications arose, and Jennifer was in danger of losing the child. She was required to be in bed, resting for the last four months of her pregnancy. As she lay in bed, day after day, Jennifer worried about what might happen to her unborn child. She worried if she would ever see her child alive. It then began to dawn on her that there was more to life than what she saw and touched in her immediate surroundings. There was a great deal more to life that really mattered which fell well outside the visible "facts" of a successful marriage or a successful career. Yes, laying in bed, Jennifer had her "wake-up call." She says she discovered "…a spiritual hunger—I just knew there was a lot more to life than I had ever been aware of and I wanted to discover what it was. I was no longer content with the status quo."

Another version of the "wake-up call" springs not from a crisis or limitation, but rather from the realization that a person's life is not turning out as he or she had hoped. I meet so many people experiencing this condition that I have labeled it "Forty and Floundering."

Take my friend Mac Bowden. I met Mac in August of 1997 while fly fishing for silver salmon in Alaska. Mac grew up in a blue-collar home in Pittsburgh, Pennsylvania. Bright, competitive, and ambitious, he climbed his way to the top of academics and sports and won a scholarship to a top university. He later attended medical school and enjoyed a career as a highly successful ear, nose, and throat specialist in Annapolis, Maryland. At forty-two, Mac had a thriving practice, a large income, a wonderful wife and family, a great house, and the time and money to fly fish around the world. But he confessed one night around the campfire, "I hate my job. I just can't stand it. I almost wish I could do anything else for a living. But I have two kids getting ready for college and I feel trapped. There really is nothing else I can do."

While I tried to comfort and encourage Mac, at the same time I laughed. I thought, *Been there, done that.* Time and again, I have seen this "Forty and Floundering." I told Mac, "When you are forty, every guy hates his job. If you are a lawyer, you want to be an artist. If you're an artist, you want to be a lawyer. It just seems to go with turning forty." Others describe their symptom as realizing you aren't going to make the big splash you thought you were when you started out in your line of work. You have a good job, you're earning a living, and you're paying your bills and supporting your family, but your life just seems a lot *duller* than you had hoped when you began on this path ten to twenty years earlier.

Travis Sheldon is a good friend of mine and a successful operations Vice President for a major corporation. Anyone who looked at his life would think, "he has the good life"—money, nice home, loving wife, great kids, economic security—but he still feels like his life and career is going to bore him to death before he gets done. "I'm not sure if I can spend another twenty years deciding where to put up paper towel holders. I really keep hoping there is something more," he explained to me recently. Like Travis, the absence of highs and lows is often enough to induce a personal crisis.

Health issues could also confront us and make us realize that there are major areas of our lives we may not be able to control. Take Bill and Rachel Mykranz; they were living life in the fast lane. In his early forties, Bill, a finance executive with a Fortune 50 corporation, was a rising star in the business world. Rachel had climbed through the ranks to reach VP Sales with Avis. She then left her career to raise two sons and, at thirty-eight, is in law school heading for a new career. Recently, the Mykranzs moved to their dream house in Cohasset, the most prestigious address on the South Shore of Boston. Life could not be better.

The "Wake-Up Call"

This past March, Bill came home with a sobering report. His annual physical revealed a growing case of prostate cancer. At forty-two, the early discovery of cancer was quite serious. His family history revealed many early deaths among the males in the family—deaths from prostate cancer.

Suddenly life took on a whole new set of dimensions. The importance of financial and career success evaporated overnight. Bill looked at his eight and ten-year-old sons, and realized his job in raising them wasn't over. As Bill and Rachel thought seriously about what the future might bring, they both realized they were facing things they simply didn't have the capacity to deal with. This situation was way over their heads. They needed spiritual resources they hadn't developed.

Most of us have reached a point in life where we have had that "wake-up call." We recognize our limitations. We discover there are many things in our life we can never control. Our lives, relationships, or careers are not turning out like we hoped. Or we experience fearful negative consequences from well-intentioned behavior. Whatever the stimulus or cause, we reach a point where we have to ask ourselves, *Is there something more to life? Is there something that I'm missing that I need to tap into? Is there a spiritual side to life that could have as much or even more impact on me than all the things I can see and touch around me? Is there something more?*

Chapter Two

SEEKING HOME

Home is a blueprint of memory. I can draw it for you. Exactly which path went where. Where the creek curved. Where my sister's pet ducks are buried. Alexandria, Virginia. 30 miles outside of Washington, DC, a place we moved to when I was 8 from Germany, where my father was stationed. Home is the smell of the wet underside of leaves behind our house—an earthy, rotting, acrid smell—and the shadow patches of cool that crossed my face like cobwebs as I ran through the woods. It is the smell of creek crayfish and thick mud after a storm. It is jumping on rocks over the creek, sometimes getting my sneakers wet, it's seeking the hiding crayfish. It's the cool of the backyard in the late afternoon. Laddie's ticks. The gutters rushing with rain during a storm. The street light buzzing on and the bugs speeding around it like I imagine the planets orbiting around our sun....[1]

Finding home is a critical step on a path to wholeness as an adult. We launch forth from our childhood home with great expectations of finding our way in the world. If our childhood home was a warm, loving, caring environment, we dream of building a better version for ourselves, for those we love, and for others in our world. If our childhood home was not what we wish it had been, we still set out in life in hopes of building a better one. No matter how poor, cruel, or even abusive our childhood environment, our hope as we set off in life is to create a better place—one where we can feel ourselves validated, affirmed, appreciated, accepted, and loved for who we really are.

My childhood home was not a happy place. In many ways, I fear I grew up a motherless child. When I think back about the memories that stand out about my childhood, they alarm me. On the surface I had an intact nuclear family: mother, father, an older brother, and a younger brother; a comfortable home in the suburbs with two cars and a dog in the yard.

I was always big for my age. Other children and adults would mistake me for a child a grade or two ahead of my actual age. I was always the tallest student in my class. By the time I got through sixth grade, I was 6'1", weighed 175 pounds, and had started to shave my beard. Other kids didn't mess with me. But I was terribly insecure and afraid.

In third grade I decided the best way to overcome my insecurity was to develop an aggressive demeanor. I found a copy of *National Geographic* with a full-face photograph of a male African silverback gorilla on the cover. The ultimate alpha male! I practiced staring down the gorilla for hours on end. Within weeks, I could stare down any other kid in my elementary school with the fierce scowl I learned from the gorilla. But I was still terribly insecure.

In fourth grade my parents sent me to the "Norristown Nuthouse" to find out what was wrong with me. I'm sure it wasn't called that—probably the Pennsylvania State Mental Hospital at Norristown, but our affectionate name for it during the days of my youth captured our sense of its real role in the community—to lock up and treat the "nutcases." Clearly I was suspected of being "one of them."

I had several sessions with a staff psychiatrist who played games with me and asked questions and had me draw pictures of my family life. Then he had my parents come in to report his findings. He told them that *they* were the ones who needed counseling and treatment—everything that was wrong with me was a result of what was wrong with them. Apparently that was not the "correct" answer. My parents left in a huff with me in tow and that was the end of our involvement with the nuthouse.

I never did figure out what was wrong in my family of origin. As a child, my favorite place in my home was a cupboard above the closet in my bedroom. This space was about 5' long, 2', high, 3' deep, and pitch black inside. I would crawl up there and hide in the dark for hours on end. Sometimes I would take a flashlight and a book with me, or I'd haul up some crackers for a snack. It was the only place in my home I felt safe. Other than my cupboard, I have no childhood memories from inside my family home.

I've been in counseling with various mental health professionals over the years, and the description of my life in the cupboard always has them running up the storm flags. I really don't know what went on. It was probably emotional abuse, but it could have been physical or sexual abuse as well. The mind has a wonderful way of burying painful memories we cannot deal with.

What I do know is that my childhood home practiced all three rules of the dysfunctional family: "Don't talk, don't feel, and don't trust." I was so insecure, I was still sucking my thumb when I was in seventh grade. Fortunately, I got braces that year, so I gave up the thumb. That was about the time I learned how to masturbate and smoke cigarettes. All through my late elementary school years, I had this reoccurring daydream. In my dream, America was involved in a nuclear war, where everyone in the country but me was killed. In my dream I'd plan how I would utilize the resources of my neighbors and in what sequence, to best ensure my survival. It was my ideal world—all the stuff in life still around, but all of the people gone!

In my teen years I began a personal quest for an authentic self. I wasn't sure what I was looking for, but I knew I didn't want to be where I was. I was looking for a new home—a new sense of self that would provide what I did not have in my life as a child. I looked in a lot of different places.

I investigated education and intellectual pursuits. At the age of fifteen, I studied existentialism and read the works of Kahlil Gibran and Leonard Cohen. I looked into romance and intimate relationships with a variety of different girls. I sought solace in cigarettes, alcohol, and the drug culture. I ran away from home for long weekends, then for weeks at a time. Finally, I reached my Jack Kerouac stage; I lived on the road, hitchhiking around America, sleeping under bridges or in bus stations, hanging out in railroad depots, and writing beat poetry in a little journal I carried.

What was I looking for? I wasn't sure. But I sensed there was a big piece missing from my life. I felt like a man with a big hollow hole in my chest. It clearly wasn't visible to the casual observer, but it was quite evident to me. The pain of this gaping hole would wax and wane, sometimes unconsciously; other times a tremendous aching in my heart that brought me to the point of tears.

My childhood experience is not at all uncommon. Many grow up in a home where one or both parents are missing through divorce, desertion, or death. It is estimated that one out of three adults has suffered from emotional, physical, or sexual abuse as a child or teen. The disintegration of the American social fabric on the altar of "success" has produced lots of adults whose childhood was somewhat less than the ideal caring, loving environment needed to produce healthy adults. I'm not the only person who feels like a motherless child. In fact, the majority of Americans may feel this way at some time or another in their life.

Just look at Judy Garland, the girl who became famous as Dorothy, the main character in the movie, *The Wizard of Oz*. In the climax of the story, Dorothy clicks her heels together and says, "There's no place like home; there's no place like home." Then she is magically transported back to her childhood home in Kansas, safe in the bosom of her warm, loving family.

Judy Garland's real life, however, was not so simple or magically happy. Garland grew up in a dysfunctional home, where she and her sisters were pushed and manipulated into various vaudeville roles to support their family. When Judy signed her first contract with a film studio, she became the primary breadwinner for her parents and sisters. From that point on, according to her daughter, her full-time job became being Judy Garland. She made nineteen movies in nine years and worked very hard trying to please everyone. But personal and career pressures drove her into drug abuse. Marriage after marriage, child after child, collapse after collapse, Garland could not "find her way home." Instead, Garland seemed to seek the place she speaks of in her famous song, "Somewhere Over the Rainbow." To paraphrase Dorothy: "Somewhere there's a land that I heard of where the dreams you dream really do come true."

Like Judy, many people feel they somehow got lost in the land of Nod. Nod is this mysterious place halfway between waking and sleeping where you find yourself wishing, wanting, and hoping for something more. What that something is, is not clear. The questions circulate: *Is it simply a larger dose of what I have now? Or is it qualitatively a different kind of stuff? What is it that's missing? What is it I'm looking for? Must I accept the scientific rationalists' view that we are in essence nothing but machines—that our loves, longings, and our deepest desires can all be explained as electromagnetic and chemical impulses?*

We want much more than to simply be a sum of dispassionate factors working themselves out in random or natural patterns in an impersonal world. The truth is, we feel there ought to be within each of us a divine spark allowing us to rise above being mere machines. This notion is the beginning of a search for home. In this search, though, home is not a physical place. It is not a place we used to live in and have fond memories of that we are trying to recapture; nor is it a future place, an ideal place we are trying to create for ourselves in this world. Home is in our hearts. The real home we seek in this life lives inside of us. We carry that home with us all the time—we don't need to strive to "arrive" there, or to go back and look for it in the past. Home is the conviction, the awareness that we are beings with a higher purpose. It is the sense that we are more than the mathematical sum of our DNA, our environment, and our human functionality.[2]

As human beings, we have an inner sense that our particular self-consciousness is an astonishing gift that sets us off from the rest of creation. Our creativity gives us a divine spark that calls us to rise above the level of a mere biological machine. We have a built-in consciousness, regardless of training and inclination, and it pushes us to ask, *Is this the right way to go? Is this the right thing to do? What ought I do in this situation?*

When we begin this spiritual search for our own place we can call "home," what is it that we are looking for? For twelve years my family and I lived in a large two hundred-year-old colonial farmhouse in central New Hampshire. It was a great old house with white clapboards offset by green shutters. Placed on a modest lawn with a large attached barn and several pastures, the property was bordered on one side by a bubbling trout stream and woods full of oaks, maples, and white birches framed by one hundred-year-old pine trees. My children spent the majority of their childhood growing to maturity in this large house, which was in all aspects a wonderful home. Recently, we sold the five-bedroom colonial and the farm. We moved into town and leased a two-bedroom condo right on the lake.

We hope this isn't a permanent move, but more like transitional housing as we ease into the "empty nest" phase of our life. My daughter, Katybeth (twenty-one years old and a junior in college) told me she was a little worried when she was anticipating "coming home" for Thanksgiving. *Would it really be coming home?* After all, we had sold her childhood home and she had never even seen the place we were now living in. Several months later, she told me, "Your new condo is still home because you guys live there. Home is where you can show up, drop all your stuff, and be yourself. It is where you aren't someone's guest. It is okay to relax, to be yourself, and to take a dump. You don't have to deal with someone else's agenda or schedule. You belong. It is being known and feeling free to do your own thing."

We are all looking for a place where we can be ourselves and be accepted. It is a place where we feel we belong. It is a place of unconditional love. We experience a measure of fulfillment and satisfaction at home; our life is full of positive meaning. We have relationships that let us know we are "home." There is a sense of inner peace and prosperity, regardless of the storms of life raging in our current circumstances or in the world around us. This inner urging, this fleeting idea, this awareness of higher issues, and this conviction of what ought to be in life is the beginning of the quest for the spiritual self. Seeking what lies beyond the mere physical components of our existence is what starts each of us on our search for home. Much of this book will share the journeys of many who have started this spiritual search. It will share the stories and principles drawn from those who are finding home, and provide ideas about how you might begin your own search for home.

CHAPTER THREE

GROWING UP LOST

I was lost. With a sense of growing fear and panic, it became clear to me: I was *really* lost. Lost in the woods. I had no idea where I was, or how to get safely out, and darkness was setting in. Having broken one of the cardinal rules of woodscraft, I realized that I was now in deep trouble... life-threatening trouble. It was my fault, but now I was trapped. As I thought about the possible consequences and outcomes, a sense of terror and helplessness began to sweep over me.

The day started out so well. Newly married, Martie and I were living in a suburb of Boston, Massachusetts. An avid outdoorsman since childhood, I loved to explore the rolling New England countryside, finding new places to hike and fish. On this splendid, crisp October Saturday, I had driven to Middlesex County to sample the noted trout fishing on the Squannacook River.

I found the stream nestled in the quaint village of Groton, home of the famous Yankee prep school of the same name. The map showed several possible points to access the stream, but only the major bridge crossing in the center of town was visible from the road. I drove several miles outside of town and parked by a woods road. Its general direction and my gut guess indicated it probably cut back to the Squannacook River. I gathered up my tackle and lunch, then hiked in. The woods road became narrower, more overgrown, and then became a path. Finally, the path faded out to undifferentiated woodland.

As a youngster, I had been a Boy Scout. In college, I taught woodcraft and survival skills for the Boy Scouts. I knew *never* to leave a path in strange terrain without a compass and a topographic map. But I was *sure* I could hear the river just beyond the trees ahead. I was *sure* I was very close. *How much further could it be?* Well, it was further than I expected, but I finally bushwhacked my way out to the banks of the Squannacook.

I had great morning fishing, catching a number of beautiful native brook trout. After lunch, a nap, and some more fishing, I was ready to go home. Heading back upstream, I kept looking for the spot I had come into the river. But the woods and underbrush looked remarkably similar. It wasn't clear where I had first hit the river. I started off back toward what I thought was the path home several times, but ended up in confusion. Nothing really looked familiar. It all looked the same!

Try as I might, I was having trouble identifying any familiar landmarks that might guide me to the path out of the woods. Now, I was on swampy ground. *What?* There was no swamp on my way in! I couldn't make sense of it. I was totally disoriented. I was lost! *Really* lost and it was my own fault.

The sun began to set. I thought of people I had known who had died in the woods from such foolish mistakes. Deciding the river was my only chance to survive, I worked back to its banks. As I went along the banks, I realized the wide sections were too deep to wade across. Finally, I heard a car pass by beyond the woods on the opposite shore! Realizing the road would eventually lead back to civilization, I found the narrowest bend in the river, which was ten to 15 feet deep. I clamped my fly rod in my jaws and proceeded to swim across the forty-yard expanse of frigid river with my clothes, tackle, and hiking boots dragging me under. Thankfully, I made it through the powerful current. Exhausted, I pulled myself out on the bank. A short hike through the woods brought me out to the quiet blacktop of a secondary road. There was no one around to help or direct me. So I picked a direction and hoped it would lead to town. Then darkness set in. It got colder and colder. After a seven-mile hike in my soaking boots and clothes, I finally arrived back at my car in the dark. I was grateful to have survived at all and happy to be shivering in my car on my way home.

Lost in the woods. That is a pretty accurate description of my spiritual condition as a young adult. The feelings I had of confusion, panic, and even terror during my misguided adventure along the banks of the Squannacook can help you understand how it felt to grow up in a world where I had no knowledge of spiritual things. I never intended to grow up in the dark, spiritually speaking. Like getting lost in the woods, it came about as a result of circumstances and choices made, but certainly not with the desire to end up lost.

I was raised in a nice suburb of Philadelphia in what I thought was a typical middle-class home. My family was essentially unchurched, although my mother occasionally attended the local Quaker Meeting, of which she was a member. My father never went to church, and the kids dropped out of the process altogether by third grade. My parents made several half-hearted attempts to teach us some values, morality, or religion without making much of a dent on our rapidly hardening hearts.

As a teenager, I began to seriously consider the purpose of life and what I wanted to get out of it. I didn't realize I was on a spiritual quest at the time, but looking back it seems this is where my search for "home" began.

Consider the era in which I came of age. President John F. Kennedy was assassinated just as I entered puberty in 1963. By the time I graduated from college, President Nixon was impeached and resigned from office over the Watergate scandal. In the twelve years intervening, the world seemed to lose its mind and spin wildly out of control. JFK's assassination was followed by Jack Ruby killing Lee Harvey Oswald on live TV. Like a lot of young people, I sat in my living room and watched. Our nation was paralyzed with the fear that the Communists were going to take advantage of our national crisis and attack or conquer our country.

In the following years, I saw the black urban ghettos in Watts, Newark, and other cities, erupt in rioting, looting, and burning. Every summer I can remember the growing fear that our country was going to succumb to anarchy from within, or the lurking threat of nuclear terror posed by the Russians. The civil rights movement spawned massive non-violent demonstrations and equally violent reactions from angry mobs of white citizens. Pictures of Americans fighting Americans filled the screen of my television every night. The Vietnam War began to escalate and claim more and more lives. News anchors reported the "body count" of the enemy in ever-increasing numbers, but the real impact came as many young American men I knew came home maimed, crippled, or never came home at all.

Student unrest broke out on college campuses all over the United States. From Berkley in California to Columbia in New York, students held sit-ins, took over buildings, and closed down the colleges they attended. "Students For Democratic Action" urged more violent resistance to the status quo. The Weathermen, Black Panthers, and other groups complied with riots, bombings, murders, and other "student actions" which culminated in the National Guard slaying four students at Kent State in the spring of 1970, as I was graduating from high school.

Meanwhile, my young friends were urging their peers to "tune in and drop out." The Flower Power movement grew into a culture of free love, drugs, and freedom from all responsibility. Haight-Asbury, a neighborhood in San Francisco, became the spiritual home for dropouts and druggies seeking an alternative lifestyle. Woodstock, where I spent four unbelievable days with three high school chums, marked the high tide of the Hippie movement before it began to crumble and disintegrate from the underlying weaknesses inherent in their philosophy and lifestyles.

On the political front, Martin Luther King was assassinated in Memphis, followed two months later by Bobby Kennedy in Los Angeles. The Democratic National Convention in Chicago in 1968 exploded into a massive and brutal attack by the police on unarmed, non-violent student protesters—all conveniently televised into the living rooms of homes across America. We watched dumbfounded as Vice President Spiro Agnew was forced to resign over corruption in office. The long national nightmare known as Watergate resulted in President Nixon's impeachment and resignation from office.

In this context, it's easy to see why I was not impressed with the conventional wisdom of my day regarding what makes for a satisfying life. These answers did not seem to be "cutting it" in the world going crazy around me.

I became disillusioned with the values of society. Prior to high school, I had been a good student, was at the top of my class, and was generally well behaved. When I hit high school, I began to connect the dots and think for myself. I did not like the picture I was seeing, and became disengaged from the educational process. My favorite phrases to describe what I was learning in school were, "trite," "boring," "irrelevant," and "redundant."

I didn't learn much in high school. In tenth grade I learned if you went out to the end of the old wing of the school, down the back steps, and out the rear exit, there was a corner you could stand and smoke cigarettes without being seen from any window, the parking lot, or the street. In eleventh grade I learned you could simply put on an attitude of supreme confidence, walk out to the student parking lot, sit in any car you liked, and smoke a cigarette in peace. The extensive view across the parking lot let you see any teacher and ditch the cigarette long before they could see you hunched down in the car. In twelfth grade I learned you could simply borrow someone's car, drive to Burger King, have lunch, and smoke as many cigarettes as you pleased without any danger of being caught. And that's about all I learned in high school.

By the time I was in high school, I knew the conventional values of society were not going to lead me into the sense of self, of meaning, of personal peace and prosperity I was seeking. I'm not sure I knew I was lost, but I knew where *not* to look to find my way home. So where did I start my search? Like many from my generation, I was convinced that the answer to all of life's questions could be found in sex, drugs, and rock and roll!

Sex is maybe the wrong way to position it. Or maybe not. I think the notion we start out with is that we are seeking a relationship to provide the sense of completion we are looking for as a person. As a guy, it was probably easier for me to confuse sex and "having a relationship." Guys often think they want sex, but what they really want is a relationship that makes them feel loved and accepted. Women, on the other hand, are often in search of a relationship and see sex as a secondary by-product of a good relationship—*or* as the required price of admission in order to have a significant relationship with a guy.

In the beginning, I was in search of a meaningful relationship with a person of the opposite sex. I met Misty Marshall on a family vacation in Maine the summer I was going into eighth grade. I enjoyed my first kiss in a wild blueberry patch on a cool summer evening as the stars came out in the crisp black night sky. We wrote each other regularly during the following school year. I poured out my heart and shared confidences I could reveal to no one else. Although I went to visit her the following summer, the geographic distance (400 miles) proved to be too much for the relationship. It eventually faded.

During the fall of my ninth grade year, I started dating Julia Payne, the second most popular girl in my grade. As fall progressed to winter and then spring, on each date we became physically more intimate. Finally in May, we both lost our virginity to one another. I was fourteen. I don't remember much about the relationship or the love thing, but the sex was great! We did it everywhere that summer—in her bedroom, behind the public pool, in the basement of her home, in the piney woods behind my house. We even did it in the moonlight on the ball field of the Catholic elementary school down the street. I don't know what we were thinking; most likely we were not thinking at all—just reveling in the pure physical pleasure of sex and believing ourselves to be in love. By the end of that summer, the limited basis for our development of a relationship of mutual support and encouragement began to show.

Sex is great, but it is not the way to build a relationship. Someone once told me that building a relationship is like tuning up a symphony orchestra. You always tune up with the violins first, then you move to the louder, less sensitive instruments until you finish with the kettledrums. Starting with sex at the beginning of a relationship is like tuning up the orchestra by starting with the kettledrums. It is so loud, it simply drowns out everything else. Sex in a relationship works in the same way. Once it kicks in, it drowns out everything else. This certainly proved true in my relationship with Julia. By the beginning of tenth grade, it was over.

The balance of my high school days saw me involved with a progression of different girls. Each relationship formed a predictable pattern. It began with the stimulation and excitement of meeting a new girl. *Maybe this was the one? The one who would provide me with a sense of worth, value, belonging, and completeness?* Many relationships would develop and often begin to climb higher and higher. Finally, it would culminate in a peak experience that would convince me that "Yes, this is the one!" Then the inevitable decline would set in. Sometimes the end came with a frightful rush, like plummeting down the highest slope at the end of a roller coaster ride. Other times the end was more gradual, like the sinking feeling you get as you walk further into the swamp, and your feet sink deeper into the ooze and mire with each step until you realize it's all over.

I have no idea how many relationships I went through in high school and college. I do know I never found the answer I was looking for in a relationship. Sometimes I found great friendship, good companions, and people I really admired. But I did not find that sense of wholeness to fill the empty spot inside my heart and soul. I knew, while a good relationship might fulfill many needs in my life, it would not help me along my spiritual journey to find the spiritual home I was looking for. I would have to look elsewhere.

The second potential answer for my friends and I was an altered state of consciousness—drugs and liquor. We were not after any mystic, transcendental, or Eastern religious experiences. In the beginning, I'm not sure we knew what we were after. But in our jaded suburban point of view, it seemed when adults wanted to have fun they brought out the booze. Business guys in gray flannel suits went out with clients for the classic three martini lunch. Housewives had the girls over for a drink of Bristol Cream Sherry before dinner. Working men stopped off at Kelly's Bar & Grill to hoist a few brews with their pals when they got off the job for the day. Any party for adults was built around a copious and free-flowing supply of liquor. We just assumed they were keeping us away from alcohol to deprive us of one of life's great pleasures. So we found ways to tap into the benefits of booze on our own.

At first it was hard to get access to liquor. So Freddie, "Chucky," and I would go uptown and buy bottles of vanilla extract. It was 35 percent alcohol, so we figured if we slugged down a few bottles we could get a buzz. One night "Chucky" and I each swallowed four or five bottles of the stuff. I don't know if it was the alcohol that made us puke or just all that vanilla flavoring, but we both got sick as dogs—especially "Chucky." That was the night he got his nickname.

Later we overcame the supply difficulties. My best friend Milt figured out he could steal a whole bottle of hard liquor from his uncle's liquor cabinet without him even knowing. There were so many bottles and so much alcohol-driven entertainment going on, as long as Milt didn't take the last bottle of any particular brand, no one seemed to notice.

By tenth grade it was even easier. Chip McVeigh's parents were divorced. He lived with his mom and her boyfriend. The boyfriend had named their cat "Dog." He christened the dog "Cat." He called Chip's mom "Lush." I was a little naive and never really understood the nickname, but years later I found out she had a serious drinking problem. Chip would host all the parties. His mom or her boyfriend would supply all the booze, which was terribly convenient. Plus they picked up the tab! We had lots of parties and the liquor flowed freely. Unfortunately, I had one of those metabolisms that just absorbed the booze with no ill effects. One night I drank an entire fifth of vodka and went home stone sober.

The only time in my drinking career I was able to get drunk was a night I'll never forget. I had been at a party with a bunch of college kids and had consumed all manner of alcoholic drinks. By this stage in my life, I had given up wanting to get falling-down drunk, so I had eaten carrots all evening to keep something in my stomach, hoping to temper the effects of the alcohol. At 1 A.M. I went home pleasantly happy, if not quite sober. At 2 A.M. I woke from a sound sleep and got violently ill. Needless to say, for many days after, I was haunted by the sight and smell of shredded-carrot vomit. The memory was powerful, and the experience began to convince me that an alcohol-induced high was not going to help me find the answers I was looking for.

Of course, there were other ways to alter your state of consciousness. While alcohol was clearly the drug of choice, there were other ways of getting wasted. After all, this was the '60s. Grass was fairly easy to obtain. Often we would hop on the commuter train to Philadelphia and troll the Greyhound Bus station and Race Street where all sorts of interesting weed and other drugs came in from across the country. A close pal and the rest of his Steely Dan Fan Club friends spent their time getting all kinds of "mood adjustment" pills. Often this led to a road that spiraled downward into coke, smack, meth, horse, and the final frontier—acid. This was serious stuff! Acid (LSD) was the epitome of hip during the Flower Power days of my youth. Unfortunately, it also had a lot of nasty side effects. Most injuries or deaths from acid were actually the result of bad behavior while "tripping." Jumping in front of trains or trying to "fly" off a bridge were typical acid-inspired stunts. Unfortunately, these behaviors also left you dead. Other acid users had nightmarish flashbacks for years. Some of my friends ended up dead because the acid they bought and tripped on was actually strychnine—a deadly poison.

I always thought taking acid was simply a different form of suicide. Richie was a classmate who went down this route to its logical conclusion. In ninth and tenth grade he partied a lot, drank a lot of booze, and smoked a lot of weed. Then he began a progression of more serious drugs. When he ran out of money, he would go down to the high school locker room and steal various things from the training supplies. Sniffing and snorting his way along in a daze, he barely managed to graduate. When I came home after my first year at college, I heard Richie had died that spring from injecting peanut butter into his veins.

In hindsight, using various drugs to alter your state of consciousness reminds me of the "Old Indian Medicine Stick" trick. When I was twenty, I ran a wilderness outpost camp for the Boy Scouts in the mountains of Northeastern Pennsylvania. Troops would come in for a week and hike to a number of the string of eight to ten outpost camps spread throughout the seven square miles of mountainous terrain. Each camp had a specialty—mine was teaching survival skills, fly tying, and fly-fishing. As a one-man staff, any injuries that did not require hospitalization were mine to take care of. The "Old Indian Medicine Stick" was a great ally in the first aid process.

When a camper would turn up with a knife gash on his forearm, I would clean the wound, disinfect it, and dress it with a bandage. At the end, if the Scout was still whimpering and complaining, I would ask, "Would you like me to take the pain away for you?"

He would look at me and ask, "Can you do that?"

"Sure," I'd reply, "I'll do it with my Indian Medicine Stick." Then I would reach under the bunk in my wall tent and pull out the Indian Medicine Stick. About 2 feet long and 2 1/2 inches in diameter, the stick was a peeled bolt of heavy rock maple covered with carvings and Indian designs. Turkey feathers, beadwork, and leather bindings completed the look at both ends.

"The way the Medicine Stick works is I roll up your pant leg and beat you as hard as I can with the Stick for a couple of minutes. When the Stick and I are done with your leg, I guarantee you won't feel any pain at all in the cut on your arm," I said.

The Scout would look up at me with eyes widened with horror and respond, "No, actually, my cut feels much better. In fact, it doesn't really hurt at all. Thanks a lot, I think I'll go now." Then he'd be gone. No more whining. No more complaints.

Using drugs and alcohol is a lot like the Indian Medicine Stick. It doesn't take away the pain you are feeling in your life; it simply masks it with a different kind of pain. Sometimes we achieve a balance for a while, where the numbing effects of booze and drugs neatly offsets the pain that comes as a part of our personal reality. But we always come back to reality, and the personal pain waits there for us, staring us in the face like an unwelcome guest in bed when we wake up in the morning. *What was I doing last night that I ended up like this?* Often our attempts to medicate our pain away through various substances create more pain and deeper problems than the original hurt itself. Not only do we not cure the original pain, we end up in a much worse situation from the "cure."

So, if the answer is not sex or drugs, is it rock and roll? The era when I made my rite of passage from being a child to a man was profoundly affected by innovations in popular music. While I was a bit young for Buddy Holly and Muddy Waters, Elvis was still shaking his pelvis when I hit adolescence. These cultural pioneers drove teens wild with joy, while simultaneously driving adults and authority figures wild with rage. What a great environment for kids who wanted to break with the values of their parents and express themselves by being different!

At the age of eleven, I can remember hiding under my sheets at night listening to the latest Beach Boys hits on my first transistor radio. In sixth grade the Beatles invasion hit America. Watching "the Fab Four" on *The Ed Sullivan Show* gave teens and adults a clarion call that a new day was sweeping across America.

I can recall almost every major incident in my teen years by dating it by a particular Beatles' song or album release. "Do You Want To Know A Secret" was the theme song for my first hard crush in the spring of sixth grade. In ninth grade I proudly strutted around town in my corduroy bell-bottoms, mod shirt with contrasting "dickie," and my rectangular granny glasses while humming the tunes from *Rubber Soul.* When I hear songs from *Sergeant Pepper's Lonely Hearts Club Band,* I connect with the feelings of lust and longing I had for Ellen, the lovely young student teacher in my tenth grade English class. Shortly after *Abby Road* and *The White Album,* the Beatles were done as a group, and so was my career as a high school student

The evolution of popular music in the 1960s was a paradigm shift of major proportions. I know, I was there. It probably had a lot to do with the massive numbers of Baby Boom children like me sweeping into adolescence. It also had a lot to do with the tumultuous times American culture and societal values were going through. The powerful economic growth and prosperity of the post World War II boom produced unprecedented financial freedom to allow these cultural trends to take place.

Joan Baez, Bob Dylan, and other folk heroes rose up out of the "beat poets" of the '50s to become a prophetic voice for this new generation. They put a voice to the fears, the pain, and the anger—the feelings of a generation. It has often been said that music is the heart language of the soul. This new generation of music gave voice to the unrest, turmoil, disillusionment, and anger felt by the tidal wave of teens rising up in America.

In junior high, almost everyone I knew was involved in a little rock band that would practice in someone's garage or basement. Each band would pick out the music of a particular hero and play their hearts out, hoping to become the next big success on the rock scene. Jim Morrison of The Doors, Janis Joplin with Big Brother and the Holding Company, Jimi Hendrix playing his famous riff from Purple Haze—these rock standouts were our heroes and role models. Before we finished high school they were all dead from the fate of their own hands—drug overdose.

Music was a major influence in my life. It was one of the first things I actually earned and spent my own money on. I would hide in my Dad's den for hours playing my albums and allowing the music to paint windows into my solitary and lonely world. Growing up in a dysfunctional home, my world was severely restricted by the unspoken but ironclad rules of our family life: "Don't talk, don't feel, and don't trust." Rock music effectively broke those rules. They put a voice to what I was feeling. They articulated the pain, the anger, the loneliness, and longing for love and acceptance I struggled with every waking hour. I was hoping music would help me find my way home. But as Steve Winwood said in his song "Blind Faith," *"...I've been wasted and I can't find my way home..."*

So how did I end up spiritually lost? Some of the causes were circumstantial. I grew up in a highly dysfunctional home. The nurture and care that should have been there was simply missing. As I look back, and as I look over the disintegrating culture in America today, it seems my experience is far more common than most would expect. In fact, it may be the norm.

The reasons I ended up spiritually lost had to do with choices I made. Seeking meaning and satisfaction from sex, drugs, and rock and roll were coping strategies that helped me deal with the pain of being lost. Like the Indian Medicine Stick, they dulled the pain or provided a measure of comfort while I continued my search. So in the end, all I knew was that I was truly lost. I wanted to find my way home. I knew somehow I needed to tap into a reservoir of spiritual resources that would go well beyond that which I could see and touch in my world. I needed to tap into my own self at some deeper, spiritual level, to find my way to a better place in this life.

Chapter Four

THE YELLOW BRICK ROAD

Pardon me for telling so many personal stories. Of course, they are the best examples I know. One of my discoveries over the years is that the people I meet also have powerful personal stories about their spiritual pilgrimage—their journeys to find "home."

My own experiences are similar in many ways to your experiences and those of others. We have stories of getting waylaid, lost, or disappointed on the journey home simply because so many of us start out with the wrong expectations. To a surprising extent, the American Dream is a compilation of myths or even outright fabrications. Our culture teaches us that, like Dorothy in The Wizard of Oz, if we could just find and follow the Yellow Brick Road to the end, all our problems would be solved and all our dreams and wishes would come true. What a crock!

Human nature, being what it is, can't help but commit to the wholehearted pursuit of whichever version of the Yellow Brick Road seems best. We make commitments and seek solutions because we want our dreams to come true, and because we hope there is something more in life than our current experience. Most of us have this sense that if we could just "get our act together," we could discover and live an abundant quality of life;

one that delivers on the wish for personal peace and prosperity.

So, like Dorothy, the Lion, the Scarecrow, and the Tin Man, we all start off following that Yellow Brick Road in hopes of having our expectations fulfilled and our dreams come true. Maybe we hope to find courage, intelligence, a feeling heart, or just a way back to the security and warmth we once knew. Whatever it is, a thoughtful analysis of people's experience reveal at least six major strategies people in America use in their search for personal peace and prosperity. Some of these will sound familiar to you. Perhaps you can see yourself in one of these illustrations.

Finding Mr./Mrs. Right

Debbie Bartlett was born and raised in a small town in southern Vermont. Growing up, she loved playing with her Barbie dolls. She was especially enamored with Barbie's relationship with Ken, the perfect man. Much of her playtime and imagination focused on her future, when Debbie would find and marry her own Ken—the perfect man for her. She was a cheerleader in high school, paid a lot of attention to her outward appearance, and focused on hanging out with the most popular kids in school. College was just a higher-level practicum in becoming the perfect "Barbie" for the "Ken" she was convinced would come along to make her life complete.

When my wife met Debbie, both had graduated from college and were single career women in Boston. Debbie was open about the fact that she was looking for a man. Her specifications were clear. He needed to be tall, good looking, blonde, and wearing a specific pattern of yellow/tan plaid slacks. This was her mental image of the man who would be the "perfect" man, the perfect husband for her.

Then she met Kent Dilahay. It just so happens Kent was tall, good looking, and a natural blonde. One day he turned up in a pair of slacks that were a yellow and tan plaid pattern—the precise pattern Debbie had always envisioned her personal "Ken" wearing in her dreams of a happy future. Not only did Kent have an uncanny resemblance to the Ken doll of her childhood fantasies, he was a graduate student at MIT. When he finished his Masters degree, he had every prospect of professional success and being able to support the type of family Debbie dreamed of.

So she set her cap for him. Kent, to be honest, was somewhat naive, as well as socially inexperienced. He was no match for a woman who had been plotting and planning for the acquisition of her own personal "Ken" since the age of four. It took a number of months, but Debbie's campaign was successful. Before a year had passed, they were married—Mr. and Mrs. Kent Dilahay! And they lived happily ever after….

Not exactly. They got married, and much to Debbie's surprise, she found she had gotten everything she had asked for. But she realized too late, she may have been asking for the wrong things. Kent had the external appearance she wanted. But Debbie began to discover that rather than turning out to be Mr. Wonderful, he really was Mr. Detached. Instead of the warm, caring relationship she expected to follow the Ken Doll good looks, Debbie found she had married a man who was incapable of forming warm, human relationships with other people. Not only was he a relational moron, there was simply nobody at home. He was successful at work, but cold, distant, and aloof from his wife and kids when he could spare the time to be home at all.

Almost before little girls first try lipstick, many have a growing conviction that if they can just catch a guy, the right guy, they will be happy and fulfilled. Boys are a little slower to develop, but eventually they catch up and begin the painful and trauma-filled search for a relationship that will bring validation and satisfaction. The pace quickens through junior high and high school. By the latter half of college, it gets pretty serious. For many men and women, they can't imagine leaving the security and predictability of college life without having snagged a marriage partner or the closest approximation of one. In a very insecure world, many view a committed relationship with an exclusive partner as the one real security they can take with them in life.

Many television shows and movies paint the expectation that the "right relationship" will be the answer to all life's problems. Many of you have discovered this is simply not true. It is fantasy, as is much of what we see on TV and at the movies. Reality tells us it is hard to get into a decent relationship with a decent person of the opposite sex. We live in a day and age where the extended and nuclear family system has been undermined, relational skills have been lost, and much sexual/relational confusion and disillusionment exists. Finding Mr. or Mrs. Right is not easy and may not turn out to be the solution we were hoping for.

Career Success

After finding the right relationship, probably the most common yellow brick road myth is that personal fulfillment comes from success in a career. How you define "career success" depends a lot on how your motivations are wired. Some can only see themselves as a success if they measure it by the yardstick of money.

The movie *Boiler Room* painted a picture of driven young men whose only goals in life came from a desire to make a truckload of money, and make it *fast*. No sacrifice was too great in the pursuit of the first million dollars. No ethical compromise was too difficult an obstacle to overcome. The accumulation of money and the material trappings it could buy was the only measure of real value and success in life. Of course, the portrait the movie paints is an exaggeration of real life. But there are many on Wall Street, in large corporate law firms or high tech companies who find themselves obsessively driven to earn large amounts of money. The rapid growth of enrollments of MBA students, law school enrollments, and other professional programs prove the popularity of this myth.

Roland and Lily Whitetower epitomize the American success story. As they tool around town in their bright red Porsche convertible or their $280,000 Bentley, they exude an air of confidence. These are clearly people who have "arrived." They have achieved a measure of monetary success that some of us will only dream of. Roland is a successful business entrepreneur. Recovering from a failed marriage twenty-five years ago, he applied himself with a partner to a new business venture. It was a fabulous success. Overnight, Roland was transformed from a struggling fifty-year-old man into a big time success. He married Lily, his executive assistant twenty-five years his junior, and retired to Hawaii where he built an exclusive retreat on the north shore of Oahu Island. Each year his earnings rolled in—usually $600,000–800,000 per year—while he kicked back and enjoyed the good life.

But his urge to create and stay involved in business never left him. He still wasn't satisfied! After ten years, he launched a new business venture. The success of this enterprise has dwarfed his previous accomplishments. Now the money is rolling in at an annual clip of ten to twenty million dollars a year, as are the opportunities to speak, influence major institutions, and have a wide variety of involvements.

The Whitetowers' success has created a feverish pitch of pressures in their lives, which threaten to wreck their marriage, their family life with their young children, and all the success the business ventures have produced. Now Roland is asking the question, "How much is enough? I know I never have to work another day in my life. But I also feel like my success has not brought the fulfillment and satisfaction that I've been seeking. How much is enough?"

Some measure career success in ways other than money. While many in professional sports and in Hollywood receive financial success, they are really motivated by fame. They want to "be somebody." They want to receive the affirmations of the crowd by being recognized and hailed as a popular (and thus important and worthwhile) person.

No One Here Gets Out Alive is the biography of Jim Morrison, lead singer of The Doors. It describes his childhood with his accomplished but austere and absent father, a career officer in the Navy. Morrison went to UCLA to attend film school, dropping out a few days before he was to graduate. With several friends, he put together a rock band that launched his meteoric rise from the Whiskey-a-Go-Go, a small club on Sunset Strip, to international stardom and fame.

At each level of success, Morrison was undermined by his self-destructive behavior: excessive alcohol and drug abuse; continuous sexual escapades and public nudity; and all night benders and violent attacks on fans, police, and even bystanders from the stage. In hindsight, it's clear that both his drive to fame and stardom and his violent self-destruction were driven by the one thing he was never able to achieve—the attention and approval of his father. At the age of twenty-eight, Morrison lay dead of drug and alcohol-poisoning in Paris.

A great many individuals enter public service as a way of seeking personal fulfillment from career success. The access to power, powerful people, and the ability to wield power encourages many to give up more financially-rewarding work to serve as appointed or elected government officials. In his autobiography, *Born Again,* Chuck Colson shares about his long climb up from a walk-up rented apartment in a working class neighborhood outside of Boston. As a "Swamp Yankee," denied acceptance as an equal by the blue-blooded Brahmins, the Beacon Hill establishment that ran the political arenas of the city and state, Colson embarked on a quest to prove his worth to those who looked down on his origins.

He clawed his way through Brown University, served as a platoon commander in the U.S. Marines, went to law school, and landed a job as an aide to a prominent U.S. Senator in Washington. After a stint in his own private law practice, Colson accepted a job as a special council member to President Nixon in 1969. Colson describes the impact that this had on him:

> As I stepped for the first time into the sun-filled, stark white, Oval Office, my heart was beating so hard that I wondered if it could be heard. I walked over a huge blue and gold oval shaped rug, the great seal of the United States colorfully embroidered in its center, directly beneath a matching white plaster seal molded in the ceiling. In front of the floor-to-ceiling windows looking out over the south lawn, the President sat at a large mahogany desk.
>
> He was leaning back in his chair, sun streaming in over his shoulders revealing the first specks of gray in his hair, intently studying the pages of a large brown leather folder propped in his lap. He glanced up, peering over reading glasses I never knew he wore, and flashed a broad quick grin: "Sit down, boy. Good to see you again. I'll be with you in a minute." With that his eyes returned to the brown notebook, on which I could read in gold embossed letters: "Daily Intelligence Summary." And below that: "The President."
>
> The President. Not the person I'd known for so many years, but the President—and in this room constructed during Theodore Roosevelt's presidency, where so much of the high drama of the 20th century had been enacted. Just to be in the room was exciting enough, but now I was here alone with the President, the single most important man

in the world, and here as a member of his staff. My life, the whole 38 years of it, was about to be fulfilled."³

Individualism

French historian Alexis de Tocqueville came from his country to study the unique culture of the new frontier for his now renowned book, *Democracy in America* (1835-39). He was so struck by the unusual character of the American people that he created a new word to describe it: "individualism." This powerful trait of the American culture persists today. "In the 1990's President Bill Clinton reaffirmed the national commitment to empowering Americans to think, decide, and vote for themselves, declaring 'In America to be an individual is our highest value.'"⁴

America has always attracted the self-starters from the population. By and large, those who have left home and traveled across the sea to settle in America have been fairly proactive personality types. "No thanks, I'm all set" or "I'll do it myself" are classic lines of the person who feels that achieving something—anything—on their own without help from others is the key to finding real satisfaction and meaning in life.

In his book *Into The Wild*, Jon Krakauer tells the story of Chris McCandless. A recent college graduate from a well-to-do family, McCandless hitchhiked to Alaska in April of 1992 and walked alone into the wilderness. He had given his $25,000 in savings to charity, abandoned his car, and most of his possessions. His earnest desire was to learn to live off the land to find meaning, purpose, and direction in his life. Four months later, a moose hunter found his decomposed body back in the Alaskan bush.

Krakauer's chilling account of this fascinating story of good intentions and unbelievably bad consequences is an apt parable of the spiritually lost in America today. Getting lost is not an intentional decision. Like McCandless, many who end up terribly lost start out with admirable intentions. But things don't work out as they hoped. Many find their way into deep trouble because they do not have critical information, or the information they have been given is simply untrue. Others make mistakes of judgment or simply make wrong choices. Often no one is around to offer them help when they finally realize they are confused, disoriented, and way over their heads in trouble. They are lost! All too often, like Chris McCandless, before they can get help and change their course, it is too late. They have made a series of choices that prove to be fatal.

Finding Friends

There are a number of ways to look at this particular version of the yellow brick road. Many of us feel that if we can connect with a group of "real people" who accept us as we really are, this will form the foundation of support we need to enjoy a meaningful and fulfilling life. When Joe Cocker sings, *"I'll get by with a little help from my friends,"* many of us perk up and say, "Yeah, that's right! That's all I need are some good friends."

David McClellan was a professor at Harvard University who studied and taught motivation. His research of human personality found that some are motivated by achievement, others by a need for power. Finally, he concluded that a large body of people are motivated by affinity. These are people whose strongest motivation is to belong. They seek acceptance and friendship from others. Rather than competing, they want to cooperate with others.

Recently, I got to see how powerful the desire to belong can be. While in Washington, DC, for a series of meetings, I had breakfast with a newly elected Congressman from Virginia. A successful businessman, he told me he paid one million dollars of his own money to win a seat in Congress. He also told me that the price was cheap; some of his friends paid five million dollars to win their seats in Congress. Then he spent an additional million to buy a townhouse in Georgetown so that he could stay in town and not have to drive the two hours to his family home back in his district.

I asked him what legislative priorities motivated him to make this investment of his money and his time. He replied, "Oh, I don't get involved with any of that stuff. I have a scheduler who tells me where to go, who to see, and how to vote on various issues. Everyone does. We really don't get involved with any of that kind of stuff." This conversation revealed that he viewed entrance to the U.S. Congress as simply joining a better club. Motivated by his desire for affiliation, it allowed him to belong to an exclusive group. The power and perks that he and his new "friends" enjoyed clearly gave him feelings of self worth he was still struggling to obtain in life.

Victoria Cruz grew up in a Catholic family, but fell away from her faith when she went to college. She married her college sweetheart, also from a nominal Catholic background, and raised three kids. While her children were all christened into the church, she and her family rarely attended. She kept looking for a way to connect to God and others, but the church told her, "Just attend the service and all your problems will be cured." It simply didn't work for Victoria.

In May of 1989, she met some young adults in Boston who seemed really excited about their religious beliefs and their friendships. She went to a couple of meetings and was impressed by the level of community they had together. Meanwhile, her marriage was on the rocks and beginning to fall apart. Victoria suspected that her new friends were really part of a cult, but she was so hungry for people who would accept her, she joined them anyway.

"It was simple, she told me. "All I had to do was give up my mind, my will, and follow all the rules of the group. It was really earning salvation and acceptance by following a type of recipe.

Do the right stuff and you have the brownie points to be accepted and loved by the group. The inference was that God also accepted you. A salvation by good works proposition. I proceeded to go through a painful divorce, but the group took care of me. That was the major benefit. Eventually, I realized conditional love wasn't really love at all. Belonging and being accepted for following the rules didn't really fill the need in my heart to be loved. After a time, my doubts and fears really took over and I fell away from the group. I still had the yearning and hunger for a personal relationship with God, but I knew simply belonging to a group wouldn't get me where I wanted to go."

Helping Others

An increasingly large number of people, especially those from the Generation-X and Generation-Y age groups, seek to find meaning by serving others. This is a noble goal and a great contrast to the often greedy and self-serving agendas of the Boomer generation.

Clint Hurt and Michelle Bowden are both thirty-years-old. Clint grew up in a very religious family. His parents were quite active in a conservative Baptist congregation. But Clint was really turned off by the hypocrisy he saw in their lives. Michelle was raised in a nominal Catholic home in Binghamton, New York. They met after college when they enrolled in a Masters degree in a counseling program at Penn State University. Clint and Michelle found themselves attracted to each other because of a shared desire to help others. The program was very rigorous and had a high dropout rate. Graduates were expected to focus their counseling career on working with court-adjudicated juvenile delinquents and their families. While the course work was challenging, both Clint and Michelle graduated with honors. Together they moved to a

The Yellow Brick Road

small city in northern New England and began their professional careers to help reach and turn around some of the most disadvantaged youth and families in our society.

The quality of their relationship meant a lot, so they took steps not to bring pressure from work home with them. Each worked in a different social agency in separate towns. Yet the frustration built to unbearable levels. After two years, Michelle and Clint were both totally burned out.

Michelle told me, "What amazes me is that most of the social agencies that we work with are far more dysfunctional than the juveniles and families we are attempting to help. The mental health field seems to attract a high proportion of professionals who are more messed up than our clients." She quit after a couple of years and now works as an administrative assistant in a large corporation.

Clint was totally frustrated by the impact insurance companies and HMO's had on his practice. "It doesn't matter what the patient needs—everything from our diagnosis to our treatment plan is dictated by an insurance company, before the client is even seen. You never have a chance to practice the skills you studied and are certified in. It's counseling by the numbers." After hanging on for three years, Clint also changed careers and now works as a manager for a software development company.

Helping others is a worthy cause. I believe the desire to help and serve others in the world around us is a God given desire which springs from the best attributes of human nature. The motivation behind this desire reflects the good intentions of those seeking community and connection with others. But by itself, as a driving force for life, it all too often falls short. The need is great, the intentions are good, but the reality of the human condition and imperfections in both society and ourselves scuttle the best-laid plans.

Location, Location, Location

In real estate, they say it's all about "location, location, location." The last major myth I want to consider is the notion that if you can just locate/relocate to the right place, then everything you want from life will fall together. This theme has two major variations. The first is that the location, which will allow me to have a fulfilled life, is one I am familiar with. This often equates to staying or moving back to the place that you know, the place that makes you feel secure and in control. The alternate variant is just the opposite. It involves moving to a different location—probably one that you really don't know at all. "If I move far away to the East Coast, to the big city, to the quiet woods, to the West Coast, to the Sun Belt… then I will find everything I am seeking in life. I will be in an environment that provides the fulfillment and satisfaction I am seeking."

Reggie Morgan grew up in Arlington, Massachusetts, a suburb of Boston. He describes his childhood home as a place of constant battles with an explosive, angry, alcoholic father. "I grew up with my fists up. I was always fighting the world or at least defending myself. I always felt afraid of the unknown. When I came home, I never knew what scary eruption might happen. I grew up feeling afraid, not worthy of love, always being judged and falling short."

As an adult, Reggie had an intense desire to be in control. He moved to Boston, went into the restaurant business, and spent years taking care of everyone else's needs. His associates at work became his substitute family—what some Generation-X analysts term his "air family." Like the "air kisses" of Hollywood's elite, the superficial non-kisses that serve as a token of real affection, Reggie's "air family" provided the stability and predictability his birth family had never been able to give him.

"I was the caretaker of everyone else's life, but too afraid to have my own life. I even went on vacation with customers from work. My world was the world I could control. I used all of my energy trying to grip the steering wheel of my life and to keep everything under control. But I found myself slipping into depression, darkness, and despair. The future held no hope for me, only the fear of impending doom."

The other variant of the "right location" theme is the desire for a different location. As a college student I read *On the Road*, by Jack Kerouac, where the author tells of his adventures traveling across America. Kerouac cuts across all sorts of characters and tries to develop some sense of meaning for his life.

Ultimately, he moves on. If the answer isn't in Denver, then maybe it's in San Francisco. If it isn't in hitchhiking with two Swedish farm boys from Minnesota hauling farm machinery, then maybe it is to be found drinking with a gal named Terri in a roadhouse on Highway 99. For Jack Kerouac, and for many of us, the great love, the great adventure, the life-filling satisfaction lies just over the next hill, just around the next bend, in the next job, or the next community. If only we could be in a different place, then all of our dreams would come true.

Like Dorothy in *The Wizard of Oz,* and like Judy Garland in real life, we wish we could find a land where dreams really do come true. Each of these six strategies for "success" has some value and may provide a measure of satisfaction. But none of them fulfills the promise of the American dream. They simply do not fill us up and make us happy. Not only haven't we found our way to our spiritual home, that place of peace and satisfaction, but we may find the benefits are fleeting, illusionary, or fall far short of what we hoped for. Sometimes these strategies leave us in a worse condition than when we first started out on our journey.

CHAPTER FIVE

RELATIONSHIPS

Reflecting on the wrong turns we have discussed leads us to a simple conclusion: there are choices we can make in life that prove to be nothing less than dead ends. When we realize our choice wasn't the yellow brick road, but a myth, a fraud, a lie, we have no choice but to turn around and go back. The end result? *Been there, tried that, hasn't worked, now what?*

Many of us, if we are honest, admit we have spent some time pursuing one or more of these blind leads but have come back to the main path in our journey through life. We aren't running rabbit trails anymore. As far as the basics go, we're in pretty good shape. At least, compared to where we used to be. Or compared to others whose lives are in a lot worse shape than ours. We've made some good choices and made some mid-course corrections. In many ways we are doing well, and yet we feel some vague sense of unease, of dissatisfaction.

So far we've described ways people take major wrong turns on the road of life and get lost. But you don't have to take a wrong turn to feel lost. Life and circumstances are like the tides of the ocean. They rise and fall, sometimes to an incredible degree. One moment your life is awash with good things, and the next it is drier than the desert. Even when the range of the tide falls within normal expectations, a surprise storm can blow into your life. The high seas which result can overwhelm your capacity to manage and lead the life you want to live. Or it can create hurricane force winds that can literally tear the roof off your life and leave you dazed and dashed in the storm's aftermath.

Our relationships are one of the two major factors that can have this type of overwhelming impact on our lives. The other, circumstances, we'll discuss in the next chapter. Relationships create the context in which each of us seek to find ourselves, make a difference in the world, and live out the things that are important to us in life.

Not to have relationships is a defining relational environment. Many people struggle with isolation and loneliness. For some, it is the result of self-induced social patterns. Many in the Generation-X and Generation-Y age groups spend their workdays in isolation and then come home to spend the evening in conversation with unseen, untouchable "friends" on the Internet. Cyber relations eliminate much of the downside of knowing people. Of course, they also eliminate almost all of the benefit of having friends and real human relationships.

Some are isolated and lonely because they have moved to a new area and are struggling to find healthy ways to connect with potential friends. Others have lost a marriage partner through death or divorce and are going through both a grieving/healing process and suffering from loneliness. In our work-obsessed culture, these conditions are not easy to overcome.

Yet even finding friends or a marriage partner will not solve all of your problems. As one wag put it, "When you are single the great question is, 'Whom should I love?' When you are married, the great question becomes, 'How can I love this person I chose?'" The problems of singleness versus marriage are different; one is not better or worse than the other. If you are married, you will discover your spouse will be unable to meet all your needs as a person. This comes as a shock to many newlyweds. Clearly one of their expectations and hopes was to have their mate meet all their personal needs. It just isn't true. It won't happen. One of the major reasons divorce rates are highest after the first five years of marriage is that, at this point, people have made this discovery, and it has so upset their perceptions about the marriage relationship, they "cash in" and try to start over again.

Married people need to develop healthy friendships with different types of people outside of the marriage relationship in order to have some of their needs met. But even a wide variety of friends and a strong marriage won't meet all of your needs. That is why you have this empty feeling in your soul, this urge to find something more—a spiritual hunger.

Even good marriages hit obstacles and sticking points. Strong marriages and struggling marriages both come to spots they can't get through without some outside help. Believe it or not, my wife and I had to get counseling over broccoli! When our kids were eight and ten years old, we kept getting into a reoccurring fight over serving broccoli for dinner. So we went to see our marriage and family counselor.

Martie's point of view was, "When I serve broccoli and he won't eat it, it sets a bad example for the kids. It teaches them to not eat a balanced and nutritious diet. He's undermining my attempts at being a good parent."

My point of view was also simple (and to me, quite compelling). "I hate broccoli! It is my home too; I earn the money to put food on the table, so why do I have to eat broccoli which I hate? I don't bad-mouth vegetables and nutritious eating to my children. I just skip the broccoli when it is served."

The counselor asked, "Are there vegetables that you like, Bruce?"

Relationships

"Sure—peas, lettuce, beans, corn, and especially cooked carrots."

The counselor asked Martie if she had ever served cooked carrots.

"No," was her answer.

The counselor asked, "Why not?"

Martie replied, "I don't like cooked carrots."

Silence fell across the room. The counselor looked at Martie but didn't speak. The color rose in Martie's face until the roots of her hair blushed bright red. The outcome of our counseling session was that Martie agreed to serve a second vegetable (like cooked carrots) when she served broccoli. Then everyone could eat the vegetable(s) they liked and no one would create a crisis for the family's nutritional values.

Periodically, every marriage needs outside help. I once heard a speaker at a marriage seminar share a profound truth. He said that when you get married, you have this ideal picture in your head of what your marriage will be like. It's a lot like the fairy tale, dream come true, picture of the beautiful bride and the handsome groom cutting the cake on their wedding day. When you look at a wedding picture you see this hopeful ideal and dream captured in a single photo. It's just the beginning of "and they lived happily ever after…"

Unfortunately, at some point, you wake up and discover your marriage relationship is quite different than your original expectation. When you go back and look at the ideal you expected (as represented by your wedding picture) and compare it to the reality of your life together, the contrast is stark and disconcerting. At the point of discovery, you are faced with one of two choices. You can take the wedding photo and tear it up (and the idealized relationship it represents); then you can go on and build a healthy marriage with the relationship you actually have. The other choice is to tear up the relationship (divorce) and go try to find the "ideal relationship" captured in the wedding photo with another person. Some people tear up four, six, or even eight marriages without ever realizing the problem isn't the marriage partner or the actual relationship, it is the false expectations represented by the "ideal" marriage photo they carry around in their heart.

If you have been betrayed by a spouse who has cheated on you, abandoned you, or divorced you, you know the pain and damage a failed relationship can bring to your life. Like an infection that gets into the bloodstream—this pain and its negative consequences can tear through your life and crop up in all kinds of areas. Pat Conroy describes his experience of divorce:

> Each divorce is the death of a small civilization. Two people declare war on each other, and their screams and tears infect their entire world with the bacilli of their pain. The greatest fury comes from the wound where love once issued forth. It was a killing thing to look at the mother of my children and know that we would not be together for the rest of our lives. It was terrifying to say goodbye, to reject a part of my own history. When I went through my divorce I saw it as a country, and it was treeless, airless; there were no furloughs and no holidays. I entered without passport, without directions and absolutely alone. Insanity and hopelessness grew in that land like vast orchards of malignant fruit. I do not know the precise day that I arrived in that country. Nor am I certain that you can ever renounce your citizenship there.
>
> ...But there are no metaphors powerful enough to describe the moment when you tell your children about the divorce. Divorces without children are minor league divorces. To look into the eyes of your children and to tell them that you are mutilating their family and changing all of their tomorrows is an act of desperate courage that I never want to repeat. It is also their parents' last act of

solidarity and the absolute sign that the marriage is over. It felt as though I had doused my entire family with gasoline and struck a match.[5]

Even with a healthy marriage relationship, there is a relational issue, which has the potential to swamp the ship of life with a tidal wave of anguish. Kids! When I was in my late twenties, I was riding from Chicago to Peoria through the cornfields of Illinois with a business associate. About seven years older than I, Phil was a guy I looked up to. He told me, "When Marie and I were getting married, we got lots of good advice about marriage—How to build a strong and successful relationship, how to love and support one another, and mistakes to avoid. But nobody ever told us when you have kids, it will destroy the marriage you just spent all that effort building!"

It was a little late to tell me this secret. My first child was due in three months! Children *do* change a marriage relationship. In essence, you can toss out the old relationship and start working on a new one. My kids have taught me a lot about myself. Some things were wonderful lessons that have made my life and marriage a much better place to live. Some were negative things—character traits of mine I've managed to avoid facing until I see them staring back at me from the sweet little face of my child. And then they become teenagers! It is true that insanity is hereditary. You get it from your kids!

Parenting is a difficult task. Many of us have too little training. We do our best, but there is no dress rehearsal. We get a shot at it and then sit back and deal with the consequences. It is no small wonder that the second highest incidence of divorce occurs after seventeen years of marriage. The stress of parenting, especially parenting adolescents, often produces enough strain to tear a healthy relationship apart.

Augusta Gone is the true story of a mother and daughter whose relationship is ripped to shreds by whatever forces cause good kids to go bad. Martha Todd Dudman tries to figure out what went wrong. Clearly her divorce and her hostility towards her ex-husband played a role. So did her daughter's choice of bad friends, and the dabbling into drugs and sex. Martha thinks she is being a decent mom, but something was unraveling. By the time she notices, Augusta, her teenage daughter, is gone.

Relationships are one of the most important contributors to a healthy life. We work, we struggle, we try again after failure, simply because it is almost impossible to grow as a human being outside the environment provided by healthy relationships. Yet, even if we have a happy marriage and healthy, well-adjusted kids, we often have a sense that some fundamental, deep-rooted personal needs are not being met. This does not mean your relationships are inadequate or in some way failing you! To think this, is to suffer from misplaced expectations.

Relationships are a means, not an end. They are not the source or cause of our growth as a person. Rather they create an environment in which we can grow as a person. The sense of falling short, or not having our deepest personal needs met, is a symptom of spiritual hunger. To fulfill our deepest needs as an individual, as a marriage partner, and as a parent requires us to tap into spiritual resources. Without a constant source of power and healing of a spiritual nature, we can never achieve the level of fulfillment we desire. Until we tap into and discover the issues of our spiritual self, we can never be all we were meant to be.

Chapter Six

LIFE IS DIFFICULT

"Life is difficult." The opening line of psychologist Scott Peck's book, *The Road Less Traveled*, captures a truth many of us have discovered for ourselves. In life, stuff happens. The unexpected, the unplanned, the uncontrollable. Events intrude upon our well-laid plans for life, pulling the rug out from under our best intentions and hopes for our present and future.

Sometimes these unexpected life events are nagging, but not life threatening—like a dull throbbing toothache that comes and goes sporadically. They're not bad enough to drive us to seek immediate attention, but they never really go away either.

In many ways, William Weld reached the pinnacle of success multiple times and then seemed to sabotage his accomplishments so he could start over again. In less than thirteen years, he quit three jobs, any one of which could have been a career capstone of a high achiever.

Born into a wealthy Boston family, he is a walking paradox: a *summa cum laude* Harvard graduate who acts like a regular guy; a lover of Latin and the Grateful Dead; a world-class charmer who can be cold and detached.

As a young attorney, he rose to become the No. 2 man in the US Justice Department. Then in 1988, he resigned over differences with his boss, Attorney General Edwin Meese III. In 1990, Weld, a seemingly hopeless underdog, captured the Republican primary and beat Democrat John Silber to become the first GOP governor in Massachusetts in sixteen years. In 1996, enjoying high approval ratings as governor, Weld set his sights on taking John F. Kerry's US Senate seat. After a heated campaign, Weld lost—a humiliating blow to his ego.

In 1997, he abruptly resigned his governorship to pursue his appointment as ambassador to Mexico. In this he also failed. His next career was to become a novelist, publishing the first of three books in September of 1998. In January of 2000, Weld left Boston to move to NYC to become the managing partner in McDermott, Will, and Emory. In this lucrative position with a prominent law firm, Weld was making over two million dollars a year. Within a year, however, he quit McDermott and his private law career to become a partner with a former client in the investment firm renamed Leeds, Weld and Company.

Meanwhile, he jettisoned his relationship with Susan Roosevelt Weld, his wife of twenty-five years, and their family. At age fifty-five, Weld abandoned his previous life and took up with writer Leslie Marshall. How to account for such chaotic behavior from one person? Weld says, "My governing passion in life is fear of boredom." His actions over the last dozen years reflect an on-going personal crisis with his fear.[6]

Others, like Scott Waddle, don't struggle with boredom or feelings of ineffectiveness, but they struggle with the consequences of poor choices, or unexpected events. At the age of forty-one, Waddle's career had experienced a meteoric rise through the ranks of career naval officers. In fact, until February 19, 2001, his career appeared to fit the Hollywood image of the perfect officer and gentleman. He was an Air Force brat who grew up on air bases in Japan, England, and Italy. In Italy he was the captain of the high school football team and President of an honors society for American students. Eager to follow in his father's footsteps, he applied to all three military service academies. He finished in the top third of the Naval Academy class of 1981.

In the military, officers like Commander Scott Waddle are "water walkers," the guys who breeze through every promotion board on their way to the top. Waddle, commander of the U.S.S. Greenville—one of the Navy's best attack submarines—had dreamed of making admiral some day. Instead, as a result of one bad day, he was sent before three admirals in a rare naval court of inquiry, which will eventually decide whether he will face criminal charges.

Engaged in an everyday test run with sixteen civilian guests on board, the Greenville surfaced and accidentally sank the Japanese trawler Ehime Maru off the coast of Hawaii. Nine people on the trawler died as it quickly sank into the Pacific. In spite of an outstanding career as one of the Navy's best sub drivers, and years of flawless service to his country, the accident will surely sink Waddle's career as fast as it did the ill-fated Ehime Maru.[7]

Sometimes we get into our chosen career and discover it is not a good fit. We may have a track record of accomplishment. It is not that we don't have the ability; we realize we simply are not motivated to do what is required. We have to force ourselves to get up; we drag ourselves painfully into the office. Often we find ourselves arriving later and later or sneaking out early, or we find so much more pleasure and fulfillment from those things we do as an avocation. Our hobbies, community service, and recreational involvements provide the real spark and joy in our lives. We wonder what life would be like if we didn't have the albatross of our job hanging around our neck.

Dennis Chang landed a great job at Dow Jones when he graduated from college. Over the course of fifteen years he made excellent progress, receiving seven promotions. With each promotion, he got increased responsibility, higher visibility in the corporate structure, and more pay. With a wife and two growing children at home, the financial rewards of his success were much appreciated.

Now thirty-seven, Chang has achieved a position of some standing in a strong, profitable, and well-managed corporation. When he meets people in professional and personal circles and tells them what he does, people's responses affirm his place is a significant one. With a lovely home (and a mortgage to match), two cars, and a family, life is good, but it isn't cheap. Even with his excellent salary, it is tough to always make ends meet with his growing family and their needs.

Yet in his heart, Dennis has a longing to dump his corporate career and give himself to his first love—a local church he helped plant a number of years ago. The church has been growing and needs his talents as an administrator. His heart is really in the expanding ministry of his church. At the same time, with his growing family's needs, it is hard to walk away from a secure job and career at Dow Jones. On the other hand, he feels he is wasting his talents by spending them on issues of the business when the needs of people in the community are so pressing. Like the boy jumping over the fence who gets his pants caught half way over, Dennis is hung up. He's torn in both directions and doesn't know where to turn to resolve this conflict in his life and career.

Women often experience mounting tension in their lives as they try to balance the demands of a solid personal life and the challenges of their work life. Many women are so busy at work, they don't have time to meet men, even though marriage is a high priority in their personal lives. Married women find that having a committed partner and a job doesn't make life any easier. Balancing all of the demands of a family and work can be overwhelming.

Journalist Amanda Ripley reports women are turning up in their doctors' offices in record numbers. "Women with jobs, children, and dinner to worry about, they tell doctors they are overwhelmed. They can't finish what they start. They are incapable of organizing their daily lives."[8]

Dr Lawrence Diller says it is tricky to know if his women patients really need drugs or just simpler lives: "The biggest problem with women is that they set the bar too high. Nobody can realistically accomplish all of these things without taking a performance enhancer."[9] They are also experiencing the prototypical lament of the modern day working mother, which sometimes makes it hard for doctors to distinguish the dysfunction from the lifestyle.

Not only can life deal us tough problems that *slowly* grind us down, but life can deal terrible tragedies in the *blink of an eye.*

Just look at the Quigleys. This was a family who had it made. Patrick J. Quigley IV was born in Methuen, a blue-collar mill town north of Boston. He worked hard to get a good education. After college, he succeeded at a number of progressively better jobs until he landed one at PriceWaterhouseCoopers in 1990. Eight years later, at the age of thirty-seven, he became a partner.

By the time he was forty, Quigley and his wife Patricia were living in Wellesley, enjoying their five-year-old daughter Rachel, and looking forward to the arrival of their second child in a month. The Great American Dream had come true for the Quigleys.

One Tuesday morning, Patrick boarded an early morning flight for the West Coast. An hour later, United Flight 175 plowed into the South Tower of the World Trade Center in New York City. In an instant, Patrick and Patricia Quigley's lives took an unexpected turn. On a large scale, he became one of thousands of victims of the most horrific terrorist attack in the history of our country. On a personal note, Patrick's life, his future, his hopes and dreams were all snuffed out in an instant, leaving a grieving widow and daughter and a fatherless child not yet born.[10]

Like our relational environment, the circumstances of life can often throw a monkey wrench into our best-laid plans. You've made good choices and worked hard; things were going well. But suddenly tragedy strikes—an accident, an illness, a job loss. You get caught in the undertow of legal problems at work or at home. Your choice of career leaves you cold, and you wish you could roll the clock back to five, ten, or twenty years earlier and make other choices. You see the chance to make a career change but are paralyzed by the potential for financial damage to your family and your standard of living. A life that seemed so on track now raises questions you simply don't know how to answer.

Chapter Seven

TURNING POINTS

A turning point comes when you are open to considering new information or perspectives. These might or might not result in a change in orientation of your life and the world, but the key issue is *are you open?* The process of exploring creates new sources of life and vitality. Like the opening of a rosebud, what once was tight and closed and hard (your inner spirit or perspective on life) now, petal by petal, opens up. It takes in new information, considers new perspectives, re-evaluates things always taken for granted. The result may or may not be a significant change in your life, but you will be a more open person, more at peace, more in touch with yourself and your world. Like the open rose, you will exude a new fragrance and a new beauty that comes with getting in touch with the things previously locked up in your inner self.

There are a number of ways of reaching a turning point in your life, but they can be classified into two groups. The first type of turning point is induced by a crisis. These are the kinds of things discussed in the previous chapters. I call these "reactive turning points." You are involved in a terrible car accident and someone you love is seriously injured or killed. You discover you have cancer. Your spouse deserts you and files for divorce. You lose a child in the eighth month of pregnancy. These reactive turning points are traumatic. In essence, you hit the wall and realize you need to toss out the conviction you had life figured out. You discover limitations. You find out you are seriously over your head and you need help. Big time!

Chuck Colson, who I mentioned in Chapter 4, had this kind of a turning point. Chuck suffered from spiritual pride. He was proud of what he had accomplished—rising from a modest family background to sit at the right hand of the President of the U.S.A. As Richard Nixon's "go to guy," he enjoyed both the exercise of enormous power and his reputation as the President's "hatchet man." But after four years in the White House, Colson found himself gradually sucked into the morass created by the burglary of Democratic Party offices in the Watergate complex. As the scandal deepened and Colson began to be pulled down the slippery slope to indictment as a co-conspirator, he realized he was in serious trouble. Colson said, "I could feel the noose tightening. There was no way to escape the demon."[11] That's a turning point.

There are certain kinds of life events, which will precipitate a crisis of meaning or belief. Each of these represents common stages in life. Almost everyone will face one or more of these events over the course of a lifetime. In most cases, their impact ranges from a significant shock, to your basic body slam, or to a complete knock out. They have the potential to totally derail your life. When one of these events happens to you, you will find yourself looking for resources beyond yourself—the true measure of a turning point. These events include:

- ✓ Moving to a new community
- ✓ Having a baby
- ✓ The death of a loved one
- ✓ Your first/last child entering school
- ✓ A change in job status
- ✓ A change in marital status
- ✓ Sickness or hospitalization

For Reggie Morgan, he had a head-on collison with a turning point. In Chapter 4, we saw how his dysfunctional family background caused him to seek to control his life at any cost. His father's alcoholic rages and volatile anger defined his childhood. As an adult, even though he was out of the home, his whole world was built around providing a safe, familiar, and secure environment. He needed this highly-controlled environment to offset the dangers he still reacted to every day.

When Reggie was forty-seven years old, his father died. In one way it was a relief. In another way it brought Reggie's life into a new crisis. His whole world was built in *reaction* and *response* to his father's anger. *Who was he, now that his father was no longer there? Did his lifestyle make any sense? Did he have any value as a person?* He found he had created a fortress to hide inside in order to protect himself. With his father gone, Reggie found he was now a prisoner in the fortress he had constructed! Over a period of several months, he realized he was at a turning point. "I really needed to redesign and restore my life from the ground up. It was clear to me; I needed to rethink my life from the beginning, now that my father was gone. My life needed to be reshaped to fit me, rather than simply react to him." This is a "reactive turning point."

A second type of turning point is much more proactive in nature. Rather than waiting for one of life's body slams to take you to the mat, this turning point involves rethinking your perspectives and priorities *before* life clobbers you.

The "wake-up call" or "reactive turning point" is like my friend, Bill, who couldn't be bothered to change his oil in his Volkswagen. When the oil problem finally caught his *full* attention, it was too late. He did notice the oil light and the engine heat light glowing on the dashboard, but he figured he'd look into it when he got home. Seven miles later, he had burned up his engine. It cost Bill over $3,000 to repair a car worth $4,000. The "proactive turning point" is like the guy who regularly takes his car in for checkups, preventative maintenance, and changes the oil religiously every 3,000 miles. It takes a little more effort, but it pays big dividends in the long run.

Knowing life will eventually deal you a body slam, it makes sense to re-evaluate before the storm hits. You probably have already sensed this, which is why you are interested in exploring God or learning more about the spiritual side of life.

Donny McClure was raised in a Catholic home. His father was in the military, so they moved a lot. His childhood was marred by his father's episodes of anger and physical beatings of Donny. As an adult, Donny figured he had outgrown all of that—until he had boys of his own. He discovered he had the same temper problems as his father had in his childhood. This revelation sent him on the road in a spiritual quest. He found a psychologist who helped him with his problems of anger in his home.

Later he went back to school to finish his college degree. Along the way, he began to reconsider what he knew about God. Much investigation led him into a vibrant, personal relationship with God. This healthy new spiritual growth in his life came at a good time, for little did he know the hurricane of pain and anguish that was about to slam into his life.

In his late thirties, Donny finished his degree and was working in a management position in his field. Riding his Harley-Davidson motorcycle home from work one afternoon, another driver failed to see him and pulled out just as Donny came past the intersection. The accident almost killed him. He had broken bones all over his body.

Donny spent the next two years in the hospital and rehabilitation. He lost his foot and the lower portion of his leg. He suffered from a variety of internal infections and depression and was living in a constant haze of pain and drugs, unable to heal, and unable to move on. Donny told me, "I'm forty years old and my entire life as I have known it has been destroyed. I have no idea what the future holds. I've often contemplated suicide. Only my faith and my daily relationship with Jesus have kept me going through all of this. I simply don't know how I would have survived without his help."

Today, Donny is well on the way to building a new life. He's learned to accept and deal with his physical limitations and is now back working in his profession. For Donny McClure, the process of growing and adding spiritual resources before the storm hit was his lifesaver!

Tracy and Clark Warshaw also had the good fortune to experience a turning point before the seas of life rose to flood level. Tracy was in her late twenties and teaching kindergarten in a local public school. She was a great teacher, a well-respected professional, and was blessed with a happy marriage to Clark. She started her spiritual search, not out of a crisis, but out of a sense there was a spiritual dimension of life she was missing. On the surface, her life was great. At the same time, there was an inner hunger, an urge to connect to God in a meaningful way she just didn't know how to satisfy. Her pleasure in her work and her satisfaction with Clark didn't seem to address this unmet need.

Tracy became good friends with another young teacher, Margo Richmond, who seemed to have a well-developed faith in God. Together they spent time exploring God and spiritual issues as they became better friends. About nine months later, Tracy found her own spiritual life beginning to blossom. As she shared her growing relationship with Jesus with her husband Clark, his own spiritual life took off. Together they both began to experience the lift of having God's resources available in their lives on a daily basis. Two years later, their only child, Amanda, began to have serious medical problems. The doctors were afraid the little girl had a medical condition that was destroying her hearing. At the time, Tracy was pregnant with their second child. Their level of anxiety rose quickly when the doctors told them the problem causing Amanda's symptoms was genetic and could be inherited by their unborn baby. Other complications developed, and at eight months, Tracy lost the baby.

It was a devastating experience for the Warshaws, but amidst the tragedy there was some light. Their own growing faith helped them through the crisis. Tracy had also become part of a small group of believers who met together to support and encourage each other. One of the other women in the group had delivered a stillborn child the year before. She was able to comfort and support Tracy and Clark with some of the lessons she had learned from her own experience with deep personal loss.

A turning point cannot only be a life-changing experience; it can be a life-saving experience. As Danny McClure and the Warshaws discovered, having started on the path of spiritual health and growth *before* the storms of life delivered a stunning blow enabled them, with God's help, to rise above the crisis and grow into stronger and better people.

At the heart of a turning point is the recognition of a key truth. We are not merely human beings. We are spiritual beings engaged in a human experience. An openness and a willingness to consider the spiritual side of our life, and not just the physical or material part of our existence, opens us up to a whole new world of richness, health, and growth.

Bruce Theilman paints a wonderful word picture of what this process is like; Theilman says we can be sun pushers or we can be chased by the sun. When we seek God's light in our lives, it is like we are facing the sun. As we move toward the sun, our shadows—all of our problems—begin to recede behind us. They get smaller as we follow the sun, as we follow God. On the other hand, if we walk away from God's light, if we flee his presence, our shadow and our problems stay right out in front of us. The further we walk from God's light, the bigger our problems (shadows) grow.

Every person is either walking toward God or away from God.

If you find your shadow and your problems are in front of you and are getting bigger and bigger, you might want to consider a turning point. Scripture defines repentance as simply stopping right where you are, turning back toward God, and beginning to walk toward his light. And so, repentance is another word for a turning point. It involves a reorientation of your life. And then most of the rest of the work of spiritual growth comes from allowing God's light and love to move your shadows behind you. Gradually, the light of his love will reduce these problems. It doesn't mean they will all disappear, but they will no longer dominate and drive your life.

Blaise Pascal (the great 17th century scientist and philosopher) reflected on mankind's fruitless search for happiness without faith and concluded that within every human heart is an infinite "God shaped void" only God can fill. In his *Pensees,* Pascal observes,

> All men seek happiness. This is without exception… some seek good in authority, others in scientific research, others in pleasure…. And yet after such a great number of years, no one without faith has reached the point to which all continually look. All complain, princesses and subject, noblemen and commoners, old and young, strong and weak…. A trial so long, so continuous, and so uniform, should certainly convince us of our inability to reach the good by our own efforts.
>
> What is it then, that this desire and this inability proclaim to us, that there was once a man of true happiness of which there now remains to him the mark and empty trace, which he in vain tries to fill from all his surroundings, seeking from things absent the help he does not obtain from things present? But these are all inadequate because the infinite abyss can only be filled by an infinite and immutable object, that is to say only by God himself.[12]

The key to spiritual growth and health is to simply turn toward God and let him begin the process. Our job is to turn toward him and be open. His job is to lead us in the process.

But if... you seek the Lord your God, you will find him....[13]

"Ask and it will be given to you; seek and you will find; knock and the door will be opened to you. For everyone who asks receives; he who seeks finds; and to him who knocks, the door will be opened." [14]

Chapter Eight

WHAT ABOUT RELIGION?

When we speak of a spiritual journey or a quest to get close to God, many people think of religion. When I say the word "religion," what pops into your heart and mind? For many of us, our instinctive reaction to that word is negative. A lot of people have had negative experiences with both religion and religious people.

I want to make it clear—there is no connection between being religious and having a healthy spiritual life. Some religious people have real spiritual health. Many do not. And a great many non-religious or irreligious people have a wonderful spiritual life. In short, religion is not the answer to your desire to grow spiritually. Let me repeat—religion is not the answer! So let's sort out the difference between religion and spiritual growth.

Two of the best-known critics of religion were Karl Marx and Sigmund Freud.

> Both men mounted a direct attack on religious faith, Marx calling religion "the opiate" of the people, and Freud calling religion "the universal obsessional neurosis." Freud concluded that God was but a projec-

tion of the childish wish for an all-powerful Father who would protect one from the unpredictable, harsh elements of nature.

Marx and Freud died in London. Marx died at age 65, in abject poverty. Freud died at the age of 83 after a long bout with cancer. Both men died bitter and disillusioned with little compassion for the common man. Freud wrote in 1918: "I have found little that is good about human beings on the earth. In my experience, most of them are trash no matter whether they subscribed to this or that ethical doctrine or to none at all."

Both had virtually no friends.... As one reads about the end of their lives—of how they finished the course—one notes an overwhelming sense of despair and hopelessness.[15]

While there are many legitimate reasons to criticize religious faith and practices, to simply throw out all hope of connecting with God is not the answer. The despair, failure, and hopelessness that characterized Marx and Freud—their lives, their loves and their last days—quite clearly illustrates the point that the response of throwing out God because of religion is not a good solution.

I certainly have had my own bad experiences with religion and religious people. When I was investigating my spiritual life and seeking better answers, I looked at a lot of things. Some, like sex, drugs, and rock and roll, were not particularly helpful. Values like education, the arts, theater, and ballet enjoyed a very positive reputation in American culture. When these didn't help, I admit, even though I was raised in a non-religious home, I was desperate enough to consider religious answers. At times I actively investigated religion. I must have really been lost and confused! I met a guy in Rittenhouse Square in Philadelphia who told me if I bought this Buddhist Shrine and chanted before it twice a day, all my deepest desires would come true. You didn't even have to believe in the process, you just had to do it. It would still produce the end results you wanted, even if you didn't believe in it. So I trudged off to a grungy walkup apartment in an ally behind Race Street and spent ten dollars on my own home shrine. I tried the discipline for a while, without having it seem to make much difference.

I met "Holy Rollers" in my hometown. In hindsight, I realize these must have been members of a Pentecostal church. On Friday nights they would cruise the streets of our town, as did many teenagers. Their goal was to buttonhole people and to get them to consider the claims of Christ. Then they would try to convince you to go with them to the Friday night evangelism service at their church in a seedy neighborhood on the edge of town. I even went with them a few times. If I was willing to give Buddha a try, it wouldn't hurt to give Christ a shot. Whether in their service or talking with them on the street, I never quite figured out what they were talking about. Not only did they use a lot of church language I didn't understand (what was all this stuff about blood, righteousness, and Ebenezers?), but their message seemed to have no connection or relevance to my life. I just didn't get it!

Research shows that I am not alone in my experience. The majority of Americans today (60 percent) do not attend church and are not particularly interested in doing so. When pollsters asked these people why they have no interest in church or religious activities, the answers varied almost as much as the individuals who are interviewed. But in general, they can be broken down into four categories.

The first reason people most often give is that what goes on in many churches is not relevant. When you ask people, "What word comes to mind when you say church," the most common response is "Boring!" Lots of people tell me, "I used to go," "I went when I was a kid," "I went but I fell asleep," "I wasn't really interested in what the church had to offer." One woman said, "My grandmother was Irish and immigrated to this country. My parents were both very strict Catholics. They made me attend and participate in all of the church's rituals. I took my own kids as well, until they made their First Communion. Then I slowly dropped away. I found what went on in the church was simply not feeding my soul."

Many people who have had some experience with the church or other religious institutions dislike the "politics" of the institutional church. They are offended by particular moral stands the church takes on issues such as divorce, abortion, and homosexuality. These issues make them feel the church is about "someone imposing other people's beliefs on me." Or they are hurt by how people in the church treat others they disagree with. When people in the church are critical, judgmental, or hateful, it is a real turn-off. It causes some to leave a particular church or religious group or to never consider them at all.

Many older generation Catholics tend to suffer from changes in the church's political positions. Raised with a strict set of values, rules, and requirements, Vatican II destroyed the traditions and mysteries of the church for many. Not that Latin Masses were understood, but the mystery made the people feel connected to God. All of a sudden, a lot of saints got kicked off the roster; they were suddenly told, "It's okay to eat meat on Friday. And you may hold to mass on Saturday. Oh, and by the way, the Pope is still infallible." These institutional changes undermined the personal faith of a lot of Roman Catholics over the past twenty-five years.

Another major reason some people do not go to church is because they've already been there. They've been there, had a bad experience, and have not been back and don't plan on going back. This group makes up much of the church-resistant population in our country today. These are not people who have had too little experience with the church, but people who have had too much bad experience with the church.

What About Religion?

Several years ago, I conducted a research study on this issue for the American Bible Society. Most of the bad experiences mentioned had to do with people-problems in the church. Here are a few quotes from people in the study who tried to describe what had happened to cause them to leave the church and not go back:

> "Two pastors were fighting for power; deacons supporting the pastors pulled guns out in the church."

> "I got divorced. When I got divorced, instead of support, they turned their backs on me."

> "The priest's homilies put down teenagers; I was a teenager at the time."

> "The preacher wanted everyone to chip in to buy his son a Cadillac."

> "The deacons didn't approve of us living together before we were married."

> "I got counseling for domestic abuse—they wanted me to go back to my ex-husband."

> "The pastor was a crook."

> "The minister came to see me in the hospital and told me I was there because I hadn't been to church."

> "Pastor was arrested... it had something to do with money." [16]

A third major reason people in the U.S. do not go to church is they have little or no experience with the church. It has never been a part of their experience in neither childhood nor adulthood.

My Dad was a kid in the '30s. His parents didn't go to church often, but they made sure Dad and his two brothers went. I asked him which church they went to. He said, "It depended on where we lived. Mom sent us to the nearest church without regard for its denomination or theology."

This was not unusual for people of the Booster generation, those born before the end of World War II. Church was an almost universal experience for most and very much an accepted part of society. This has not been the case for those born after the war. For many Boomers and Busters, they simply have had no exposure to church, except for the odd wedding, funeral, or family occasion. As adults, however, they would no more think about hanging around in a church than they would think about hanging around in a graveyard.

A last critical reaction to church is caused by a negative perception of institutional churches. Religious people, in general, tend to have very negative images today. When you talk to teenagers, they often tell you religious people are "stuffed shirts," "old people," "your grandparents!" or those who "get all dressed up and pretend." Adult friends tell me they feel religious people don't have any fun in life.

My friend Teresa calls them, "bun heads," a phrase that conjures up a straight-laced ramrod back, a too-tight hairdo, a sucked-in face, and frowning attitude. A person wound so tight, any evidence of life strikes them as an offense to God. Not only do they transmit a holier-than-thou attitude, often they are hung up with long lists of "dos and don'ts." For them, their religious faith involves rules—rules you keep, rules you break, and rules they use to punish people who break their rules.

I don't want to pick on any one religious group on this issue. Lots of them demand conformity to a wide assortment of hard-to-justify rules. This religion "by recipe" also tends to drive away thinking people.

Before she got to know God, Teresa was afraid if she explored God, she would have to toss her brains out. She found out it wasn't true. A genuine relationship with God invites questions and doubts and dialogue. He invites an active intellectual participation in the journey of spiritual growth and faith. Religious rule

What About Religion?

books have the opposite affect on intellectual life. They tend to extinguish it.

The religious approach can induce a lot of guilt and anxiety. One of my best friends growing up was raised in a strict Catholic family and attended the local Catholic elementary school. Vince went to confession and mass every week, fasted for Lent, and did all the special holidays. In short, he was taught to follow all the rules. As a kid, I loved to climb trees in my yard and to build tree houses. Vince never could join me in these activities. His parents had told him to climb a tree was a sin. I don't think the church actually taught this, but his parents labeled everything they didn't want him to do as a "sin." But sure enough, the only times Vince ever tried to climb a tree, he fell out and hurt himself. He spent most of his childhood in a state of anxiety and guilt about all the rules and his failure to keep them. In his early twenties, he got so depressed, he went home, took his belt, and hung himself in his closet. My view is that he died from religious guilt.

One doesn't have to look far in history to find strong evidence religion has been the cause of widespread suffering and harm. Islam, which is currently in the news for the violence and terrorism spawned by its fundamentalist sects, has a long and bloody history. Since its founding in the early 600s A.D., opposition (both within and outside the faith) has been treated at the point of the sword or gun. The Crusades (1095-1291) were launched by European Christians against Muslims. The Christians of this era, however, saved their worst for their own. The Inquisition (1231—1559) persecuted perceived enemies within the Roman Catholic Church. As it spread, it caused massive waves of abuse and harm in many of the so-called civilized countries of Europe.

Simply picking up the newspaper provides regular examples of the negative impact of religion and religious people. Rev. Jerry Fallwell weighs in against the Muslims saying, "The Muslim faith teaches hate." When asked if community faith groups with Islamic ties should be able to receive federal funds under President Bush's faith-based initiative, Fallwell replied, "Islam should be out the door before they knock." Not that Fallwell is narrow-minded in delivering his invective. In 1999 he accused Tinky-Winky, the purple cartoon character on the kid's TV show "Telletubbies," of being gay because he carries a purse.

Bigotry and hate are not limited to Christian religious groups. Louis Farrakhan, the incendiary black minister who heads the Nation of Islam, has long been noted for his angry rhetoric, which is anti-white, anti-Semitic, and anti-establishment. According to *The Washington Monthly*, this fiery extremist has long been suspected by both blacks and whites of involvement in the assassination of his predecessor, Malcolm X.

The Sikhs are a religious sect founded in opposition to the caste system of Hinduism, the majority religion in India. While they practice many personal religious disciplines, they also have a long record of fierce violence toward those of other faiths. Against a background of frequent religious riots causing thousands of deaths in India, extremist Sikhs assassinated Prime Minister Indira Gandhi in 1984, launched a civil war in the Punjab in 1987, and were accused of masterminding the 1985 bombing of Air India Flight 182, which crashed into the Atlantic, killing 329.

Perhaps what we dislike the most about some religious leaders is their hypocrisy. When we think of Jim and Tammy Faye Bakker soliciting donations from little old ladies and using them for a $7,000 air-conditioned doghouse, it really bothers us. Of course, Bakker's sexual behavior was also disturbing, especially when he was preaching Christian morals from the Bible on national TV everyday. In 1987, Jim Bakker and the leaders of the PTL Club went to jail for defrauding PTL viewers of more than $150 million.

What About Religion?

In 1988, Jimmy Swaggart, an Assemblies of God minister with a large national TV audience, was photographed with a prostitute. In 1997, Rev. Henry J. Lyons, President of the National Baptist Convention (the largest association of black churches in America), used his position to bilk businesses and philanthropic organizations out of four million dollars. Marital infidelity brought down Mr. Lyons, convicted in March 1999 on grand theft and racketeering. The whole ugly business came to light when Mr. Lyons' wife burned down the $700,000 home Mr. Lyons purchased with his alleged mistress.[17]

Former speaker of the House of Representatives, Newt Gingrich, became a leading spokesman for family values and an ardent leader of the impeachment attack on President Clinton over his sexual misconduct with Monica Lewinsky. After resigning from office, Gingrich ended his own eighteen-year marriage to pursue a six-year old affair he'd been carrying on with congressional aide Calista Bisek. Louisiana congressman Bob Livingston would have replaced Gingrich as Speaker of the House, but in late 1998 he admitted to multiple adulteries and resigned from Congress. Even Representatives Henry Hyde, Dan Burton, and Helen Chenoweth were exposed with old hidden affairs while leading the Clinton impeachment in Congress.

The Rev. Jesse Jackson was gracious enough to provide "spiritual counsel" to President Clinton to help him recover from his "moral stumble" and to repair his marriage and family relationships. Several years later, supporters were stunned to learn the fifty-nine-year-old black minister had been carrying on an extramarital affair with a thirty-nine-year-old employee of his Washington office. Rev. Jackson's mistress, Karin Stanford, was in the process of delivering his secret "love child" at the same time Jackson was providing pastoral counseling on morals to the President.

The astounding hypocrisy and bad behavior of religious people and their leaders is not a new phenomenon. Two thousand years ago,

Jesus had a lot to say about religious leaders, not much of it positive. He told his followers regarding the religious leaders of his day, "But do not do what they do, for they do not practice what they preach. They tie up heavy loads and put them on men's shoulders, but they themselves are not willing to lift a finger to move them."[18]

Jesus went on, "Woe to you, teachers of the law and Pharisees, you hypocrites! You shut the kingdom of heaven in men's faces. You yourselves do not enter, nor will you let those enter who are trying to."[19]

"Woe to you, teachers of the law and Pharisees, you hypocrites! You are like whitewashed tombs, which look beautiful on the outside but on the inside are full of dead men's bones and everything unclean. In the same way, on the outside you appear to people as righteous but on the inside you are full of hypocrisy and wickedness."[20]

In conclusion, let me make it clear I am not trying to say all forms of religious expression are bad. Neither am I writing off all religious people. What I want you to understand is there is not a connection between "being religious" and having a healthy spiritual life. Some people who are religious have great spiritual health and a strong relationship with God. Their lives exhibit all the positive fruit that comes from knowing God in a personal way. But there are just as many non-religious people or irreligious people (like me) who also have healthy spiritual lives and a positive personal relationship with God. The point of this chapter is quite simple: if you have negative feelings towards religion, religious institutions, and religious people, you are in good company. Many others do and for very valid reasons. But having negative feelings toward religion need not exclude you from actively exploring God, developing a personal relationship with him, and experiencing the benefits of a healthy spiritual life. The balance of this book is designed to help you to learn how to do that—to explore a relationship with God without getting religious.

Chapter Nine

A RELATIONSHIP WITHOUT RELIGION

When I was a girl, although no one in my family was religious, I prayed every night. I remember folding my hands and waiting for what I then called "god" to arrive. Inside my mind, I saw a stage—a curtain behind my eyes—then the curtain opened. I saw the presence of something that I remember as a deep, velvety black would appear and I would feel comforted. I spoke to this presence about my worries, my hopes, my fears, and my dreams. It was at these moments that I felt my heart open. I could speak freely—I asked that everyone I loved would be taken care of, that I would do well in school.[21]

Georgia Heard, author of *Writing Towards Home,* shares something all of us long for deep in our hearts. We long to be connected. We have an intense desire to belong, to find our way home, to be in a relationship. Each of us, even if we have had no religion in our upbringing, has a yearning to be known, accepted, and loved. Just as we are.

Arthur Smith shares what it was like to be an orphan from infancy:

> I was found in a basket in Gimbals (a New York City department store) on the 12th of January 1918. The people who found me called the police who called in the welfare people. They estimated my age to be a little over a month. So they arbitrarily gave me a birth date of December 2. They gave me the name "Arthur Field" and then had me baptized Protestant. I was nurtured in the Nursery and Child Hospital in New York City. Then I was bounced around in whatever foster care program they had. I was never in one place long enough to have any sense of belonging in any way, shape, or form.
>
> At the age of five, the Children's Aid Society began to prepare me for a trip... the only thing that was explained to me was that I was going to ride on a train to find a family and a home. I didn't have much of an idea of what home was, but it sounded like the ideal thing. When we arrived in Iowa, we were taken to a Methodist church. I don't remember too much; things were happening awfully fast. I'm afraid I was in that state of bewilderment where I was just going along with the program. Probably, it was a good thing.
>
> I was a lonely little boy because I had nobody that I could call my own, either other children or adults. I must have been told to go up to someone and ask them if they were going to be my daddy, because that was what I did. I climbed up on a man's knee when we arrived. I put my arms around his neck and I said, "You gonna be my daddy?" I guess I must have been a pretty good salesman because that man wound up being my daddy.[22]

A Relationship Without Religion

All children and all adults share the same dream Arthur Smith had. We dream we are not alone in this world. We feel a desire, from birth, to be connected to other people, to be connected to the world in some meaningful way, to be connected to God. This yearning for relationship is quite natural. We were created to be in relationship. God made us to be in relationship with each other and to be in relationship with him.

> In our hearts we crave nothing more than to become authentic persons, to become intimately relational, to be repentant, to be forgiven, to enter life abundant and eternal. And yet, modern existence diminishes and dissolves the person into his components, has no room whatever for repentance, never seeks forgiveness, and as for life eternal, this existence "lives" only for the moment, or at best for the near future.[23]

The great majority of adults in America today profess a personal belief in God. According to pollster George Gallup, 86 percent of American adults say they believe in God. Another 8 percent say that they believe in a "universal/higher power." Knowing there is a God and being able to connect with God in some sort of meaningful relationship are two quite different things. How can you get into a growing relationship with God without getting hung up in all the negative aspects of religion? The heart of the issue comes down to the difference between "having a relationship" and "being religious." These are vastly different things.

Religion is a man-made attempt to get into contact with God. When people realize their estrangement from God and are finally ready to seek him, they often turn to various religious systems to try and make connection. In essence, we try to rely on our own efforts, our own power, and our own goodness to earn points with God. It is as if we think by doing good deeds or by performing various rituals, that we can please God and earn our way into the positive relationship we desire with him.

Armand Nicholi, MD, a professor of clinical psychiatry at Harvard Medical School, talks about how universal this feeling of needing God is among even the most non-religious people:

> Everyone experiences the feeling of worthlessness to a greater or lesser extent. If we peer beneath the surface of the most egotistical person, we find that his/her conceit covers deeper fears of inadequacy and incompetence. College students with the highest academic performances frequently harbor the constant, deep-seated fear of being unintelligent. One sometimes also finds these feelings of inadequacy in older adults who have been immensely successful. Some people are able to use these fears adaptively, to work excessively hard, and to achieve more than they would without such fears; however, with most of us these feelings incapacitate and discourage us.
>
> Whatever the cause of our feelings of worthlessness, the important question is how we ought to handle them. Some are paralyzed by them—avoiding all activity that involves risk of failure lest they fail and confirm what they feel about themselves. Others work hard to disprove their feelings. And some handle feelings of worthlessness by projecting them. People have the tendency to see others, especially others who differ from them, as worthless or inferior. This sort of judging goes on and on. Perhaps all of this is but a desperate attempt to cope with our own feelings of inadequacy and worthlessness.[24]

Religion is our attempt to deal with these feelings of worthlessness, the need for forgiveness, the desire for relationship and meaning. Religions are systems, philosophies, or myths created by humans

A Relationship Without Religion

in an attempt to deal with our sense of separation and needing God. But at the heart of each religion and all religious enterprise is the notion that by applying ourselves diligently to a set of beliefs or rules, we might earn our way into a relationship with God.

When you think about people who are into church, you think about their expectations: attend church regularly; more is always better; the best churchgoer is the one who goes to church most often. You ought to subscribe to various theological creeds and doctrines of the church. You need to adhere to the behavioral rules of the church (don't drink, dance, smoke, play cards, go to movies, or hang out with girls/boys who do). You should give money to the church, buy a candle, or say a certain number of "Hail Marys" or "Our Fathers."

In the Hindu religion, one life is not enough to atone for the mistakes of a person.

> The law of Karma—that whatever wrong we do we will have to pay for in some other life—rules out the very idea of forgiveness. According to the law of Karma, reincarnation is therefore necessary in order to pay for the sins of a previous life. One's present life is determined by one's previous existence, while ones' future existence is shaped by one's present life. Each soul is held to be responsible for its own destiny. The law of Karma offers a simple and attractive explanation of the mystery of suffering in the world. People suffer because of their own evil actions.[25]

Several Melanesian religions encourage adherents to walk on beds of live coals in bare feet, also known as fire dancing. This "act of faith" is supposed to be a way of repenting and suffering for one's sins in this life. Buddhists, like the Hindus, also subscribe to a life of meditation, wisdom, discipline, and personal denial in order to earn their way into higher and higher forms of existence until they reach perfection and release from the endless rounds of birth and dying. Morality, generosity, holy day observance, pilgrimage, and social responsibility all contribute to earning your ticket out.

The Mormon religion was founded by a failed farmer in upstate New York in 1840. Mormons are most often known for their long adherence to polygamy. They believe only men may be members of the church; women are saved through their husbands. They claim God has evolved from man and that a person's future is determined by their actions in this life. Only members of their group will make it to heaven, and they consider all other Christian churches apostate.

Like the Mormons, the Church of Scientology is a new religion. It is quite popular with some of Hollywood's stars, including Tom Cruise and John Travolta. It was founded in 1954 by L. Ron Hubbard, an American comic book and science fiction writer. Hubbard claimed to have visited heaven twice and returned with the ideas for his religion, which actually started out as a series of self-help courses. Adherents follow a practice they call "auditing," where one member holds two metal cans attached by wires to an electrical instrument called an "E-meter." The unconnected member asks the other probing questions while the E-meter sends a small current through the body which is supposed to detect the "energy and mass" of suppressed emotions and spiritual angst.

Scientologists believe they must understand their own spirituality to reach "the supreme being" which is not one god but a spiritual being of your own choice. By attending (and paying for) many courses (which are very expensive), practitioners can learn to audit and purify their lives.[26]

Even Jesus concludes religious efforts simply promote laws created by humans and pretend that they are God's will.

> Some Pharisees and teachers of the law came to Jesus... and asked, "Why do your disciples break the traditions of the elders?"... Jesus replied, "And why do you break the command of God for the sake of your tradition?... You nullify the word of God for the sake of your tradition. You hypocrites! Isaiah was right when he prophesied about you: 'These people honor me with their lips but their hearts are far from me. They worship me in vain; their teachings are but rules taught by men.'" [27]

Religions are created by humans to develop a set of beliefs and behaviors we hope will help us work our way back into a meaningful relationship with God. The powerful desire for such a relationship is good and part of the human condition. Religion is not the answer, however. It is doomed to fail because it is based on our best efforts—which are never enough and never will be enough. In the final analysis, religion's "dos and don'ts" are no better than the Boy Scout approach, "Do a good deed each day and you'll be all set." It is great to help an old lady across the street, but it is the worst kind of wishful thinking to hope this will get us connected to God.

If religion is not the answer, what is? God himself supplies the answer. The central key to the puzzle of spiritual life and a relationship with God is that it is not something we can do for ourselves. It is something God initiates and he gives us the answer as a free gift. Jesus explains God's purpose for us. "I have come that they may have life, and have it to the full" [28]

God created us. He created us with a spiritual nature and a longing to be in relationship with our creator. He created us for abundant life. Each of us is created with a special purpose, what Frederick Buechner calls, "that place where our deep joy and the world's deep hunger meet." God wants us—each and every one of us—to discover what it means to be fully human; to be spiritual beings who are on a human journey; to allow us to enjoy knowing himself; to discover our best selves; and to live out that special purpose we were created for both now and for eternity.

God knows our separation from him, our isolation, our loneliness, our pain, and our despair. He takes the initiative to connect to us. Dr. Nicholi, the Harvard psychiatrist mentioned earlier, shares his own experience regarding faith and worthiness:

> Does faith in God provide resources to help deal with feelings of worthlessness? I think so. Once again the starting point for me is the full realization that in and of myself, as far as my relationship to God is concerned, I could do little to improve my worth. But this realization does not lead to despair, for I recognize that my worth is not in what I do or in what success I achieve. The Scriptures state that my worth is in what God has already done for me. "Not by works of righteousness which we have done but according to his mercy, he saved us. It is the gift of God."[29]

God loves us not because we are worthy, but because he finds us worth loving. It is in his nature to reach out to us with love, much like a loving father with a small child. We love our children, not because of what they do for us or how they respond to us; we love our children *before* they can even respond to us. We love our children *in spite* of what they do to us. And God loves us even more and loves us perfectly; he is love personified! Let his healing and love for you wash over you. It is not something you have to do; it is something that he chooses to do for you.

God takes the initiative. Throughout recorded history, we see the living God intruding into the world he created to re-establish a relationship with his children. God called Noah and established a

A Relationship Without Religion

relationship with him and his descendants. He called Abraham, Isaac, and Joseph, wandering Semantic tribesmen in the desert, and established a relationship with them as well. He called Moses, the prophets, and the kings of Israel.

God is constantly reaching out, initiating, and healing the breach in his desire to have relationships with his children. He goes so far as to send his own son, Jesus Christ of Nazareth, into history, into *our* world to build a bridge back to God that would stand for all time and for all people. Jesus is alive today, and he is the bridge back to the loving, healing relationship with God we all long for.

Jesus explains God's purpose in sending him to us:

> "For God so loved the world that he gave his one and only Son, that whoever believes in him shall not perish, but have eternal life.... He who listens to you listens to me; he who rejects you rejects me; but he who rejects me rejects him who sent me.... I have come that they may have life, and have it to the full.... Come to me, all you who are weary and burdened, and I will give you rest.... I am the resurrection and the life. He who believes in me will live, even though he dies; and whoever lives and believes in me will never die.... If you hold to my teaching, you are really my disciples. Then you will know the truth, and the truth will set you free.... When a man believes in me, he does not believe in me only, but in the one who sent me."[30]

> Such is the inscrutable way of God. He takes the initiative from the other side without consulting us. This is how he graciously surprises us, keeps us off balance from our perch of self-assurance. This is how our sense of wonder is kept freshly on the alert, in order that we may give thanks, ascribing nothing to ourselves.[31]

We don't need religion. We are longing for a relationship, not rules and regulations. We need a relationship with a living God who can set us free, who can help us discover our true and best self, and who can help us know him and to help us enjoy his love for us forever.

> What we desperately need is not thinking about God, about Jesus Christ, or about the Holy Spirit, but these themselves. Thinking about them becomes a poor substitute for living them.[32]

When Jesus spoke to real people in the real world, they would often,

> wander off into some anxiety, some fear, some doubt and uncertainty, some darkness—all perfectly human and perfectly natural. And time and time again he would bring them back to face the truth—namely to face him, himself. He told the world in effect, "The truth is I myself—not philosophy, not the law, not some vague theory, not human reason, not some human technique, not even so called life and activity, not even my teachings and my acts." But this was so astonishing that people often "changed the subject"—wandered off into something else. He would not let anyone change the subject. For anyone to get stuck short of him was the greatest tragedy and the most egregious sin. In fact to him, sin was not at all what we usually call sin—he forgave all that—but simply and only being away from him. So in effect, he would tell his listeners, "Here I am, right here—and you are still seeking something else?"

> What is really new is the embodiment of the living truth in Jesus Christ, not ideas or systems or theories or even theologies. There is no end to these things, and they

all more or less regurgitate the same thing (the failed strategies of trying to reach God on your own efforts).[33]

God is initiating in your life, in your inner voice, in your spirit; he is calling you to himself. He wants to give you his love—for free!

Here's how he did it in my life: During the summer I was vacationing in Ocean City, New Jersey. One evening I tried to pick up a cute girl sitting on a bench looking out at the waves. We struck up a conversation, and she started to talk to me about Jesus and having a relationship with God. I was primarily interested in the potential for romance, but I had thought a lot about the meaning of my life and the purpose of life.

"Moffit" was a good church-going girl from a middle-class suburban home. She had entered into a personal relationship with Jesus the year before. She was as much interested in finding out what a "hippie poet" thought about God as she was in sharing about her own faith in Jesus. We struck up a conversation that went on, or I should say off and on, over the next two weeks. I would make some progress toward understanding the "God thing" and then I would take off for another adventure. The funny thing was I kept running into Moffit, and God kept our conversation going.

This process culminated one morning when Moffit finally said, "It's like this, Bruce. When you look in the mirror at your life, what do you see? If you like what you see, fine—no problem. You are on your own. If you look in the mirror, and you don't like what you see, you can give your life to Jesus. He will keep all the good things in your life. The bad things he will throw out, and he will replace them with his good things."

As I left her family's house and walked down the street, I glanced in the mirror at my life. I really didn't like what I saw! So I knelt there on the sidewalk, and I gave my life to Jesus Christ.

That was over thirty years ago, and I am still walking with him. He is still in the process of tossing out the bad things in my life and replacing them with his good things.

What attracted me was not a religion, not a system, nor a set of rules. What attracted me was a relationship, and the potential for a relationship with God that dealt with negative issues in my life and built upon the positive things that were already in place.

God is alive and you can know him today. He is initiating and calling you and me into a personal relationship with him. Not religion, but a relationship with him will provide the answers we seek.

SECTION TWO

MAKING REAL SPIRITUAL CONNECTIONS

I find that most people today are restless and hungry

to get "into the game" and experience

the deeper meaning of their lives.

~Ken Blanchard

Chapter Ten

GOD WITH US

If God had a name, what would it be? And would you call it to His face? If you were faced with Him and all His glory.... What if God was one of us? Just a slob like one of us? Just a stranger on the bus, trying to make His way home?

In her song, "One of Us," Joan Osborne articulates a feeling many of us have had. It is so hard to relate to God! A cosmic power who created and controls the universe is hard to relate to if you are just one finite, limited person—like you and me. It would be so much easier to relate to God, to get to know him, if he were... well, like one of us.

In the prophesies of Isaiah, we are told that God would be sending a messiah, or a savior, whose name was "Immanuel," which translated means, "God with us." Isaiah, Jeremiah, Ezekiel, Daniel, and other prophets foretold the coming of God's son throughout 800 years of Old Testament biblical history. These prophecies are fulfilled in the historical person of Jesus of Nazareth.

God took the initiative by coming into our world in the form of a person, his son Jesus Christ. God did this because he knows we need help in relating to him and his love.

In human form, Jesus is the fullness of God's character. Scripture tells us that Jesus is *fully God* and *fully man*. How can that be? To be honest, I haven't the faintest idea. It is all too big for me, but I can trust God in spite of mysteries I cannot fathom. I know that God is big and powerful, but I need to connect with him in a size and shape I can relate to. Jesus makes that possible.

Jesus is God's "show and tell." When I was in third grade, I would bring into my class a turtle or a salamander or wild flowers to try and share with the other kids something of my love for nature. In the same way, God sent Jesus into our world in order to share a little something of himself with us in a way we can relate to. He came into our comfort zone and spoke to us in terms we can understand. He shares a little taste of his love, compassion, healing, power, and truth in the person of Jesus. He still does so today. This is the essence of what we call "the Incarnation," namely, God with us.

The facts of the Incarnation are fairly simple to understand; however, they are, radical and life changing in their implications. God is in the business of intervening in our world and in changing lives, even today. The way he has chosen to do it is through Jesus.

Jesus was born of a young virgin named Mary in a poor working class family in the Middle East about 2000 years ago. He lived to the age of thirty-three and had a significant teaching and healing ministry for the last three years of his life. He was crucified as a criminal, died, and was buried. Then, three days later he rose from the dead. He appeared to over 500 people over a period of forty days after his resurrection. He then ascended into heaven to sit at the right hand of God the Father and left the Holy Spirit (the third person of God) to do his primary work here on earth. These facts are easy to learn from both followers and secular historians of Jesus' day.

Why would God go to all this trouble to intervene in our world in this rather unique and unorthodox way? We find a clue to God's dilemma in Scripture. In the beginning, God made all things, both the heavens and earth, all the plants, animals, men, and women:

> Through him all things were made; without him nothing was made that has been made. In him was life, and that life was the light of men. The light shines in the darkness, but the darkness has not understood it.[34]

God created the world, created mankind, and he desires to have an on-going relationship of love with every person he creates. Yet he is frustrated because we, both as individuals and as a human race, have rebelled and decided to do it on our own. We want to be independent—make our own decisions and choices. In short, we'd rather be god for ourselves, thank you. Separation from God is how Scripture defines "sin." It is not something you do; it is something you choose to be. It is trying to be god in your own life or in the life of another.

So how can God bridge this separation? He made us and yet he lets us choose. We choose to ditch him and the relationship with him, and we suffer the consequences. We want to connect and to know God, but the gap is too great.

The solution is Jesus. God sent his son, Jesus of Nazareth, because he cares so much for us and wants to reconnect and be in relationship with each of us. The Incarnation is God's compassionate response to our situation. In Jesus we find the God who is willing to come to us, to hang out with us, to be our friend and our savior on terms we can understand.

Jesus was a real historical figure, but he is also alive today. With the Holy Spirit, he demonstrates God's commitment to be available to us twenty-four hours a day, seven days a week. He is truly *God with us*.

So why did God choose this particular way to come into our world? It seems like a pretty drastic, even unlikely, strategy to reconnect with your lost children. I can only speculate, but two thoughts come to mind. First, God may have chosen this approach so we can be sure that it is really God who is doing it. I'm not so sure if I was God, I would have chosen to come into my world as a tiny helpless baby, born of an unwed virgin girl in a poor conquered Middle Eastern country ruled by Rome. Everything about Jesus' conception, birth, and life seems to be just the opposite of what we humans would think of as a good world intervention strategy. I mean, birth by a virgin? That's not possible! Well, it is not *humanly* possible.

I clipped an article from the *Boston Globe* a few years ago. It describes a woman named Jill Shields who fell from 10,500 feet. She was skydiving and her parachute didn't open, and she fell to the ground in some swampy muck in rural Geauga County in Ohio. She had some bruises and minor fractures, but essentially walked away from the accident without any serious injuries.[35]

Now our response is, "That's not possible!" Of course, it's not possible. It totally contradicts the laws of nature. But it actually happened. With quite a few eyewitnesses. All of whom agreed it was a miracle.

Just last week I heard a news story about a teenage girl in a nearby town who fell out of the back of a pickup truck. She landed on her head and died. Now we say, "That's a natural consequence. That's the laws of nature at work." So how could you fall 10,500 feet and walk away from it? I don't know, but it happened.

The virgin birth is similar. It's not humanly possible, but it's clear God intervenes and acts in ways contrary to the laws of nature when it suits his purposes. When you read the accounts of Jesus' birth and life, it is apparent God acted in a way that makes it very obvious this was not a deal created and orchestrated by men. It's something only God could do.

The second reason God may have chosen this strategy was to ensure that we wouldn't be tempted to take any credit for what God has chosen to give us. God's gift of a second chance through Jesus is free. *No* strings attached. "For it is by grace you have been saved, through faith—and this not from yourselves, it is the gift of God—not by works, so that no one can boast."[36]

Jesus tells us that if we believe in him and trust our lives into his hands, he will give us abundant life today and eternal life forever. He promises a new birth, a spiritual birth, and it depends entirely on him and not at all on ourselves. There is nothing I can do to add to God's grace and to facilitate the process. God says, "If you seek me, I will find you."[37] There is nothing my best efforts can do to help God help me. It is a free gift. It is not based on any merit or worthiness on my part. We aren't worthy—that's why it is grace.

My dictionary defines grace as: "Favor or mercy shown without regard to the worth or merit of the one who receives it and in spite of what the same person deserves." Grace is most powerfully revealed and given in the person of Jesus Christ. By his life, death, and resurrection, Jesus restores the broken relationship between God and his people.[38]

Scripture tells us that our attempts to be righteous are worthless. The most accurate biblical translation would read, "…all our righteous acts are like filthy menstrual rags…"[39] Not a pretty picture.

So, give it up. Forget about it. For those of you like me who are problem solvers, drop it! God doesn't need our help to do this deal. Not at all. So, just sit back, accept his free gift, and learn to enjoy the ride.

Jesus is one with the Father. Along with the Holy Spirit, he is part of the creator God who made the universe and sustains our world today. John 14:6 says he is the way, the truth, and the life. He is the personal embodiment of grace and truth. He tells us that he is our good shepherd, our advocate before God, our way to connect into a personal relationship with God. Jesus is also our healer, the great physician who ministers to our physical needs. He loves us now and forever; he helps us bear good fruit in this life; and finally, he brings us into eternal life with God forever.

When Jesus was raised from the grave, he met with his disciples on a number of occasions. He explained that while he was going to live at the right hand of God the Father, he was going to send the Holy Spirit, the third person of the Godhead, to be with us forever. Jesus said the Holy Spirit is the spirit of truth whose job is to be our personal counselor, to teach us the truth, and to remind us of all that Jesus said. He is our comforter in this world of pain and turmoil. He gives us wisdom, prompting us in our decisions as we seek God's guidance in our lives. It is also his job to convict the world of sin and to convince them of the forgiveness and new life offered in Jesus.

The power of the Incarnation is that God loves us so much he sent his only son, Jesus, to come into the world to teach us how to reestablish a personal relationship with our loving, heavenly Father. God loves us so much he allowed Jesus to die on the cross to pay the penalty for our sins. He loves us so much he raised Jesus from the dead so he could be our advocate before the Father and be available to us always and forever. He loves us so much he chooses to live in us through the Holy Spirit, so we might continually know his love, guidance, comfort and power in our daily lives.

The Incarnation is God's chosen way to work with us, his people, in this world we live in. Incarnational strategy is God's strategy to reach people. In history, he did it through the life, death, and resurrection of Jesus Christ of Nazareth. In the spiritual dimension, God now acts through the risen Christ and the Holy Spirit to be available and active in our lives and in our world—24/7. Yet the most interesting manifestation of the Incarnation today is that God chooses to accomplish his will on earth and in people's lives through his Spirit living and working through ordinary people—ordinary people who do extraordinary things because of their relationship with the living Jesus.

Now those of you who have watched the TV series, "Touched by an Angel," can imagine the advantages if God chose to do his work here on earth exclusively through angels. Angels don't get hungry, they don't get tired, they don't screw up, they can appear and disappear at will, and they know what people are thinking and feeling. Hey, this sounds like a much more convenient and effective strategy, if you ask me.

But it is not the one God has chosen to use. Instead, he has chosen to accomplish his work on earth through ordinary people—people like you and me. People who are friends and followers of Jesus are the team of people God has chosen to accomplish his will on this earth. It is already truly amazing that God's love is alive and active in our world today, but it is even more amazing that he reaches out and touches people's lives in extraordinary ways through ordinary people like you and me!

When we become a friend of Jesus and start to walk with him, God adopts us into his family forever. Not only do we become sons and daughters in his family, but he also puts us to work in the family business! He allows each of us to become the means of delivering his love and grace to others in this world.

Chuck Colson, who we met in Chapter 4, shares how God used a business client to help him connect with Jesus. In the summer of 1973, back in private law practice, Colson felt his world caving in on him. His exit from the White House, the mounting legal pressures of the Watergate scandal, and his loss of interest in life itself were overwhelming him. "Many men I knew encountered periods like this in their life," Colson recalls, "especially in their 40's—fears about the future, about self-worth, 'male menopause'—it's often called."[40] Colson kept going through the motions but really suffered from high levels of anxiety and depression.

He stopped in to see Tom Phillips, the President of Raytheon. Phillips was a very successful executive at the electronics manufacturer. He went to work for Raytheon after college and military service, rising rapidly to the top. At the age of thirty-seven, he made Executive Vice President, and at forty, he was promoted to President. He had done this with hard work, day and night, non-stop. Phillips told him, "The success came all right, but something was missing. I felt a terrible emptiness." Colson shares,

> Phillips was boggling my mind. Life isn't worth anything, when you are the President of the biggest company in the state, have a beautiful home, a Mercedes, a great family, probably a million dollar salary?...but he had struck a raw nerve—the empty life.[41]

Tom Phillips invited Colson to his home. Over iced tea on the porch, he went on to share his own experience of meeting Jesus and accepting his free gift of grace. He shared with Chuck and helped him to confront his own need, his pride, and his genuine desire for a personal connection with God. Over the course of the next several days and weeks, Chuck Colson began a friendship with Jesus that would radically change his life for the better forever.

If you want God to be active and present in your life, like Chuck Colson did, you can simply ask him to send you or to connect you with people who know and love Jesus. If they are friends of Jesus, they have Jesus himself living inside, they are indwelt by the Holy Spirit, and they have access to God's love and power and can share it with you.

Now let me warn you: no follower of Jesus is perfect. Far from it. They are all broken, sinful, hurting, wounded human beings; and in many ways they may be no better off than you are. But because of their relationship with Jesus, they have a unique channel to access God's love and power. Don't expect these people to be perfect, or even better than you or others, but do recognize they can help you connect with God in a personal way, if that's what you want.

God is at work today in people you know. They may be co-workers, or neighbors, or relatives. They may be people you've known for years or people you pass by and never notice. They may be very outspoken in their conversation about Jesus, but most are not.

Most are getting to know God. He is gradually changing their lives in Jesus, and they are quietly loving and caring for people around them. They may not engage in overt "God talk" with you, yet I'm sure God has his people right at hand and accessible in your life. That's the point of the incarnational strategy. God wants to be available to you in your world 24/7. You don't have to go to him. You just have to ask him to reach out and find you. He's standing right next to you even as you read this book.

How do you find these friends of Jesus? First ask Jesus to help you connect to one or two of his people. Just talk to Jesus like you would a friend. Close your eyes and talk as if he is sitting in the chair across from you. I know this is a bit experimental and may feel odd, but try it. It can't hurt you. You have nothing to lose—and everything to gain. Ask Jesus to help you meet some of his friends so you can get to know him. Then begin to look through the people you know. You see, friends of Jesus have hope. If you know someone who has a lot of hope, ask them the reason for their hope. Followers of Jesus have been told to, "Always be prepared to give an answer to everyone who asks you to give the reason for the hope that you have."[42]

Also look for people whose lives show evidence of love and compassion for others—people willing to serve others and put others' needs before their own. Jesus says, "No good tree bears bad fruit, nor does a bad tree bear good fruit. Each tree is recognized by its own fruit."[43] Another indicator is how people handle the storms of life. Those who know Jesus have an inner strength and calm that allows them to face tragedies and obstacles. My friend Teresa eventually found a relationship with Jesus through her friendship with Peter and Nancy. She watched them through the death of parents and other dear ones and saw an inner strength and resilience she wanted in her life. It led Teresa to ask questions, explore the issues, and eventually to take her own first steps of faith.

Keep asking Jesus to point you to the right person(s) to talk to. We are told, "If any of you lacks wisdom, he should ask God, who gives generously to all without finding fault, and it will be given to him."[44]

Chapter Eleven

I'M A MESS, YOU'RE A MESS, BUT IT'S OKAY

Most of us, deep down inside, don't think we're okay. When we are honest with ourselves, we admit we don't need help coming up with a long list of personal shortcomings. In our inner most being we actually feel we are unworthy creatures with grave faults.

At the age of seventeen, I was a typical adolescent—big, tall, strong, but sporting a heavy case of pimples, harboring a lot of fears, and in general, suffering from free-floating anxiety and low self-esteem. I did love the outdoors and spent many hours cruising the woods and meadows behind my house. Stalking along with my .22 caliber Marlin rifle, I often walked for hours—sometimes, searching for small game to harvest for the dinner pot; other times, just exploring for the pleasure of seeing what lay around the next bend.

One bright fall afternoon, I was easing my way up a wooded ridge when I heard voices coming over the next knoll. Moving closer, I discovered three younger boys down in the canyon, the commuter railroad tracks which cut through the ridge I was on. This canyon sliced through the ridge walls, leaving steep rock walls about 40 feet high with space enough at the bottom for a pair of bright steel rails carrying passenger trains from the suburbs into downtown Philadelphia. The boys were busy piling large rocks on the tracks, I believed, in a naive hope they would de-rail the train when it came through.

Faulty thinking is not common in seventeen-year-olds. I decided my job was to be a good neighborhood vigilante and scare them off from their misdeeds. I raised my rifle in the air and fired off a warning shot. To my horror, I watched as two of the three boys stopped and looked around, but the third boy crumpled onto the ground, curled up into a ball, and cried out, "I've been shot!"

All I could do was stare in amazement. *I only shot up into the air—How could I have shot a kid 40 feet below me on the tracks?* In a panic, I turned and fled through the woods.

Arriving home, I hid the gun under my bed and tried to act normal and innocent. The next day, police started to move up and down the street, interviewing residents and looking for information to help solve the shooting.

In my senior English class, we were reading Fodor Dostoevsky's *Crime and Punishment,* a story about a guilty character living in constant fear, alarm, and expectation of discovery. That is exactly what I was going through. On one hand, I wanted to do what was right and turn myself in. On the other hand, I could envision myself spending the next ten years in prison for manslaughter.

My life as I had known it was over—no college, no future, no hope. I'd made mistakes before. Lots of them. I'd done things I was embarrassed about, even ashamed of, but this was a whole different experience. With one unthinking, well-intentioned action, I had ruined my whole life. If I turned myself in—jail and a ruined future awaited me. If I didn't, I knew that my conscience would punish me far more than any penal system could.

My faith in God was young, but I harbored a hope he was interested in the affairs of my life. As I considered my dilemma with him, I felt his urging to do the right thing. In the end, I decided it would be easier to suffer the negative consequences of my foolish behavior than to live a lifetime with the searing guilt and recrimination I was suffering from my conscience. I turned myself in.

The police took my statement. I went to the hospital to visit the injured boy. It turned out the bullet hit an overhead transmission wire and ricocheted down into the pass, hitting him in the knee and leaving a small flesh wound which soon healed. I asked his forgiveness and that of his parents, which was freely given. The police, after taking my statement and talking with both families, never pressed charges, nor was there any permanent record of my misdeed. In short, God was gracious to me. He didn't let me reap the natural consequences of my action. He didn't simply dispense justice; he didn't even stop at mercy. He gave me grace—undeserved favor.

Many of us, when we first consider the fact of God's offer of restored relationship through Jesus, have a response which leaps immediately to our lips: "I'm not worthy of his help and attention." Even when we are in a foxhole and the whole world is shooting at us and we are in such deep trouble our very life and future are threatened, we are reluctant to call on God for help. We don't feel worthy of his attention and help.

Sometimes this is the result of a lousy self-image or low self-esteem. If people in your life who are close to you have given you negative feedback rather than love and affection, you most likely suffer from this malady. Others have lived with critical parents—no matter how hard they've tried, how hard they worked, or the level of success they achieved, they can never earn the approval of their critics.

That was certainly true in my case. The fact I had a tendency to lie, steal, manipulate, and control other people may also have had a role in lowering my self-esteem. One didn't have to look long at my behavior to see a whole slew of misdeeds which caused me to feel bad about who I was and who I was becoming.

I'm a Mess, You're a Mess, But It's Okay

Dr. Nicholi, the Harvard psychiatrist talked about earlier, says others suffer a sense of worthlessness and depression because of a perceived gap between who they feel they are and who they feel they ought to be. "What often appears to be the cause of despondency in many today is an awareness of the gap between what they think they ought to be and what they feel they are. There is a discrepancy between an ideal they hold for themselves and at times think they measure up to, and an acute awareness of how far short they fall from the ideal."[45]

When I am honest, I admit I am a mess. When you are honest, you probably feel on some level you are a bit of a mess, too. All of us, no matter how successful, accomplished, talented, and "together" on the outside, are periodically aware of our brokenness, our faults, and our need for healing on the inside.

So, I'm a mess; you're a mess, but it's okay! It's okay because God responds to our condition with his grace. In God's economy, grace is the fact that in Jesus Christ, God gives us what we need, not what we deserve. We need and want a second chance. We need and want to reconnect into a relationship with God that helps us to grow spiritually. We need and want to tap into his spiritual resources to help address the areas of need and failure in our lives.

Are any of us worthy of a second chance? No. We all fall short. We fall short of our own standards for ourselves, let alone God's standards for us. We are all guilty of turning our backs on God and wanting to live our own lives independently, being a god unto ourselves. None of us is worthy, but God doesn't offer his free gift of grace in Jesus because we are worthy. He offers it because he loves us.

> Love is patient, love is kind. It does not envy, it does not boast, it is not proud. It is not rude, it is not self-seeking, it is not easily angered, it keeps no record of wrongs.

Love does not delight in evil but rejoices with the truth. It always protects, always trusts, always hopes, always perseveres. Love never fails.... And now these three remain: faith, hope and love. But the greatest of these is love.[46]

God loves us not because we are worthy. None of us are worthy. He loves us because it is his nature. He created each of us in love. When we turn from him and go off in our own way, he still loves us. He loves us no matter how far we run from him and how deep into the pit of pain and error and failure we fall. He never loses sight of us. He never stops loving us. And he never stops reaching out to us to try and pick us off the ground, dust us off, and help restore us to a relationship with him.

When my girls were young and trying to learn to walk, it was fun to watch. They would hold onto my leg or the sofa and, hand-over-hand, they'd try to tug their little body into an upright position. When they were finally standing, they'd look at me and beam with pride in their accomplishment. Then they would let go of their prop, take a wobbly step or two, until they lost balance and fell into a heap onto the floor.

So what was my reaction? Did I scream at them, "You fool! You fell down! Can't you walk like a normal kid?" Did I whip them or beat them for their failure? Did I get up and walk out of the room and abandon them for their failure? Of course not! I reached out, picked them up, dusted them off, praised them for trying, kissed their bumps, and encouraged them to try again! And how many times did I do that? *A lot* of times! And did I ever give up on them? No. Eventually they learned to walk.

If I, a sinful, human father, can exhibit that kind of love and patience with my children, what makes you think your heavenly Father who created you and continues to reach out to you is going to have less love and patience with you? He wrote the book on love.

He wrote the book on grace. He is offering you a fresh start and a personal relationship with him through Jesus. It's a *free* gift. All you have to do is accept it.

Bill Hybels gave the best description I've ever heard of God's grace. It goes something like this: You are at home enjoying the morning and sipping coffee on your patio on a quiet suburban street. Down the street, the fifteen-year-old son of a neighbor is cutting school for the day and hanging around the house while both of his parents are at work. He decides to take the family's car out for a spin. Slowly, he backs out of the driveway. As he starts down the street, he begins going way too fast. Tires smoking, he panics and loses control of the car. The vehicle races across the street, cuts the corner of your driveway, clips off your mailbox, tears across the lawn, smashes through 20 feet of white picket fence and landscaping, then comes to rest in the flowerbed at the edge of the patio where you were enjoying your coffee.

What is your response? You know the family has been having trouble. There has been a good deal of tension in the marriage. The fifteen-year-old boy has been struggling at school with his grades. The father lost his job a year ago and only recently has found new employment and is beginning to recover financially.

Yet, it is up to you. What is the appropriate response? Here is what justice would require. You march out, collar the kid, and drag him into your house. You call the police to come and record the accident and book the kid for reckless driving and driving without a license. You call the parents to make sure they "throw the book" at him in case the courts don't, and you demand financial restitution to replace the thousands of dollars of ruined property. That is justice.

Or, you could respond with mercy and not justice. You could collar the offender, read him the riot act, but you don't call the police. Having an arrest record won't make his present or future any better. It won't help the situation with his family. Instead of demanding financial compensation to repair the damage, you let him work it off. You agree to pay for the materials if he will come over and rebuild the fence, mailbox, and repair the damage to the lawn and plants. This would be showing mercy.

There is a third response—one of grace. In this scenario you run over to the car and open the door while asking, "Are you okay?" You help him out of the car as he blubbers his apologies. You say, "It's okay, it's only stuff. I'm just so glad you weren't hurt." You take him into the house, calm him down, and give him some milk and cookies. When he has recovered a little, you help him back his car off your lawn onto the street. You tell him not to worry about the damage—you'll have it taken care of. Not only don't you call the police or report his misdeed to his parents; you invite him out to lunch. At lunch you draw him out, ask him about his situation at school and at home, and try to build a relationship that provides the support and nurture he needs to get through a difficult patch of adolescence. This last response is grace—not what we deserve, but what we need.

Grace is God's response to us. It is not what we are worthy of. It's not a fair response to where we are in our lives. It's not even mercy. It is way beyond that. God gives us what we need. He reaches out with his love and forgiveness and reconciliation through Jesus. He offers to restore our relationship with him, to forgive our wayward lifestyles and all our misdeeds, wiping our slate clean and giving us a fresh start and a second chance. He offers love, friendship, spiritual resources, his presence, and continuous help in the daily details and concerns of our lives. To this relationship, we bring only ourselves.

Yes, we may be a mess, but it's okay; Jesus will do the rest.

Chapter Twelve

TWO WAYS TO HEAVEN

At the age of forty-seven, Amelia Torres had a busy and fulfilling life. Married to her high school sweetheart, mother of two girls and a boy, she had a great family life. For a number of years, she served as an educational aide in a local elementary school and was well known and respected in the community. On Sunday, November 15, 1998, she went to church in the morning and came home for lunch. After lunch, she took off her shoes and stretched out on the couch for a nap, while her family dispersed in a variety of directions to enjoy the late fall afternoon. At 4:15 P.M., her husband Joe arrived back home to find her still on the couch. But she wasn't breathing. She was stone cold and had apparently been dead for several hours.

I don't know why death is always such a shock. Sometimes it arrives suddenly, other times with agonizing slowness. We know with 100 percent certainty, death is an experience everyone of us will go through—yet we often seem totally unprepared. Among those standing in the long line of hundreds of mourners at Amelia Torres' funeral, many were people my age (late forties). And many were saying, "I was so shocked. I thought death was only an issue for older people. I never thought it could happen to somebody my age!"

The next time you are standing in line at a funeral with friends, ask them, "Are you planning on heading north or south when you die?" They will know what you mean. Most will say, "North, I hope." Then ask them on what *basis* they hope to spend eternity in heaven, rather than hell. The typical reply might be, "Well, you know I may not be a Mother Teresa or anything, but I'm not a murderer either, and just because I don't go to church every Sunday doesn't mean I don't believe in God or live a pretty good life. I suspect I'm somewhere in the middle of the pack. I hope the good deeds I have done will outweigh the bad deeds over the course of my lifetime and I'll get in. Say, God does grade on a curve, doesn't He?"

My friend David Morgan has given the best explanation I've ever heard of God's requirements for letting us into heaven. David, a pastor, shares,

> The Bible says there are two ways to get into heaven. The first is by performance—by how you live your life, by your good deeds. In theory, you can work your way into heaven. The second way to heaven is abandoning the first and trusting instead in Jesus and what he has done for you on the cross in paying the price for your misdeeds. If you choose the first way—to get in on your own merits through performance—the Bible says you only have to do two things to get in. Two simple requirements.[47]

David, a baseball buff and a Red Sox fan in addition to being a pastor, uses his favorite sport to explain God's requirements for earning your way into heaven by a life of good deeds:

> First, you must live a sin-free life. That means error-free living. This means not one sinful thought, not one sinful word or deed, not one slip-up your whole life. The

second requirement is that you must get a hit every time you're up at bat. You must have a continuous display of righteousness every minute of every day of your life."[48]

In order to meet God's high standards to get into heaven, you'd have to be like a major league ball player, playing his entire career error-free (no throwing errors, no wild pitches, no getting picked off, no fielding errors) and batting 1.000 every season for your entire career—a hit every time at bat—not one strike out, not one fly out, not one ground out.

The standard God sets for admission into heaven is high:

> If a person could live their whole life error-free, always doing what is right, and other centered in every way, every day in thought, word and deed, then he or she is in. They have kept the law perfectly and God will say to them on judgment day, 'Welcome to heaven! You were incredible, just flawless! I've never seen anything like that!' Do you know of anyone who has a perfect record, is error-free, who bats 1.000 every day?
>
> Only Jesus. In fact, Jesus is the only person in history who lived a sinless life, an error-free life, and a totally righteous life on this earth.[49]

When you study the standards God sets for admission into heaven in the Bible, it's really quite sobering. Most of us hope we can do more good things in life than the bad we are aware we have already done. But then we realize God's holiness means it's not a matter of doing my best. Nor is it that the good stuff outweighs the bad stuff. Based on God's standards and his requirements of perfect, error-free living, we all fall short of the mark.

The Jews in Jesus' day were transformed by learning this revolutionary truth for the first time. Before Jesus, their whole belief system was based on the law and on an elaborate set of rules. Jesus taught them they would never make it that way—the bar was set way too high. It was statistically impossible.

It's the same today for the Jew or Gentile, the Muslim or Christian, the colored or white person, the short or tall, the fat or skinny, the rich or poor—*everyone*. "For all have sinned and fall short of the glory of God."[50] Morgan concludes,

> We all fall short and all of us have committed errors. No one makes it this way. You see, that is good news! Simply acknowledge you don't measure up and there is no way you can make it on your own. By coming to this realization and accepting the simple truth about ourselves—we become eligible to receive the free gift of salvation made possible through Jesus Christ (the second way to heaven).[51]

Abandon the hopeless pursuit of better life performance statistics. Put your trust in Jesus and trust in his free gift of forgiveness, redemption, and a new, eternal relationship with God.

Glenn Loury taught economics and public policy at Harvard after receiving his PhD from MIT. Dr. Loury, who has a long string of academic honors and achievements to his credit, shares how his life was transformed by learning the difference between trying to build a life on the merits of his accomplishments rather than trusting in God's gracious gift through a relationship with Jesus:

> The fact is that I have been born again. I was dead and now am alive, not because of my own recuperative powers, but due to the power of Christ to mend a broken life, to "restore the years that the locusts have eaten." Let me explain; although a wonderful and beautiful woman loved me and had agreed to become my wife, I was unable and unwilling to consummate with her the relationship our

marriage made possible. I was unable to be faithful to that relationship. I am not speaking now only of adultery; I was unable to be present emotionally. I was unable to set aside enough of my selfishness to build a life with someone else. Marriage involves give and take, but I gave little. My pride and a self-centered outlook eliminated any chance for a fruitful union.

I was dead in spirit in spite of the fact that I had professional success as a tenured professor at Harvard. What more could one ask for? I had reached the pinnacle of my profession. When I went to Washington, people in the halls of power knew my name. I had research grants. I had prestige. Nevertheless, I often found myself in the depth of depression saying, "Life has no meaning." I would say this out loud with so much regularity that my wife came to expect it of me.

This is not to say I was suicidal or psychotic; I was not. For me, there was no real joy. My achievements gave me no sense of fulfillment. Nothing in my life had any sense of depth or meaning. I thought of myself as living on the surface of things. Life seemed to be one show or contest after another in which I had hoped to score high, to win accolades, and to achieve financial gains. But there was no continuity, no coherence, and no thread of meaning, which gave these various achievements ultimate significance.

Moreover, I was in slavery to drugs and alcohol. I don't want to be overly dramatic here; this "enslavement" had been going on for many years without apparently impairing my ability to function. There was no sudden degradation of my condition. I did not go off to shoot heroine between seminars or anything quite so sordid as that. I don't want you to envision some terribly ugly or desperate and sad experience though it became in due course quite sad enough. Rather there was an ordinariness about this dependency. The fact is, I thought I needed to intoxicate myself in order to enjoy an evening's entertainment, to enliven a visit with my family, to have fun at a party or a sporting event, and so on. This pattern had become part of my life and had progressed eventually to the point of threatening both my health and my name. Yet through it all, I never thought there was a problem.

These developments in my life eventually came to a point, where without some intervention my marriage probably wouldn't have survived.

After a friend suggested Loury was quite literally "walking through the valley of shadow of death," he began to consider the course his life had taken and its ultimate destiny. One Sunday he wandered into a church service and heard a sermon on redemption. Loury shares his reaction:

> I wept quietly for two hours, thinking about all that I had done for which I needed to be forgiven. At the time, I didn't acknowledge to anyone, not even myself, that I was being touched by the Spirit of God.
>
> There was no one particular moment when the skies opened up and God came wafting down. Rather, over the months as I began to study the Bible, as I went to church, as I learned to pray, as I began to reflect honestly on my life, and as I began to open myself up to the Spirit of God to minister to me and to move me, I came to realize that there was something dramatic missing in my life. I realized there was an explanation for the low condition of my life. The many things that seemed out of line were all connected to the spiritual vacancy I was becoming aware of.

Moreover, I began to feel myself growing and changing. I began to be aware that there was something real to this Christian business.[52]

Loury's life illustrates a powerful principle: no matter how stellar our accomplishments in life, they are never good enough to outweigh the mistakes, the shortcomings, and the failures we have experienced. I think most of us, when we are brutally honest with ourselves, realize that. We tend to avoid making an honest evaluation because of the fear and panic it may induce. It's too hard to confront our own failure when we fear there is no cure, no forgiveness, and no hope for a better future. Jesus provides us with the way of transforming our failure into a future with hope. Through his free gift of new life and new relationship with God, we can be forgiven of our past mistakes, the slate wiped clean. In Jesus we are given a new start—a second chance—in fact, a third, fourth, fifth, etc., as many chances as we need to learn to get up and walk through life with him.

When you understand God's requirements to get into heaven, you realize the futility of trying to get there based on your own performance. Jesus offers a way out and a way into hope for the future. He says, "I am the way, the truth, and the light. No one comes to the Father except through me." He also said, "I am the door [into new life].... I am the river of life. The only way to find true satisfaction is through drinking of the springs that I supply."[53]

That is good news! That is tremendous news! It's life-saving and life-changing news!

Section Three

EXPLORING THE LIGHT

I wanna be in the Light

As You are in the Light.

I wanna shine like the stars in the heavens.

Oh Lord, be my Light and be my salvation

'Cause all I want is to be in the Light,

All I want is to be in the Light.

~Charlie Peacock

Chapter Thirteen

THE GOOD NEWS

I was in California a few years ago and was invited to a meeting at the Crystal Cathedral, a large church in Orange County. In this Monday night meeting were perhaps fifty people of varying ages who had recently met Jesus and were involved in a growing relationship with God. Perhaps a dozen guests, like myself, had been invited to sit in on the session that evening. At one point, the moderator asked if anyone wanted to share either how they had met Jesus, or what difference he was making in their life. A number of people shared, but I will never forget what one man had to say.

He looked to be in his early thirties and was clean, well dressed, a nice guy. The man got up and started to share about his life. Everyone in the room was transfixed. He talked about sliding downhill from a promising start into a nightmare of relational and moral failures, substance abuse, personal failures, and pain. The previous Saturday he had gone out on a bender. Sunday morning he woke up and found he had passed out in the living room of his apartment. Turning on the TV, he saw a service from the church.

On an impulse, he got in his car and drove to the church. He met some people who started a conversation with him. Eventually they introduced him to Jesus. Forty-eight hours later, he stood in the midst of this group and said, "I don't know what's happened to my life. But I do know I have been radically changed! I came into this place yesterday morning and I was a loser! Now, I know Jesus and I am a winner!" With that he sat down.

I was stunned by his statement! That is pure minimalist theology. The brevity took my breath away: "I was a loser. Now I'm a winner." Yet as I looked at this man, it was perfectly clear he was filled with the Spirit of the living God. He had been transformed. He glowed with God's presence. There was no doubt that even though he could not explain what had happened, God had done work in his life and the man would never be the same.

Over the years, I have discovered that God is very tolerant and open-minded. He does not object to minimalist theology. Or California theology. Perhaps you don't live in southern California. You may be from one of the many other cultural variations that weave together to make up the social tapestry of the United States. This message about God's love is so important, I want to be sure I have communicated it clearly. Bear with me and I will try to lay out the basics of how you can have a personal relationship with God in terms anyone can understand.

So what is the good news? *Jesus* is the good news; the good news also referred to as the gospel. The word "gospel" is from the Greek word "euaggelion," which translates as "good news" in English. While some think of the gospel as a set of concepts, doctrines, or theological truths, it is much more. It is God's truth about getting back into a relationship with him, embodied in the life and person of Jesus himself. Jesus is the gospel. He is the truth and the principles of God's reconciling love acted out. He is also the person who will be our friend and will walk with us through life, both now and forever.

How can you connect with Jesus and begin this process of walking in his light? It's really quite simple. Perhaps the best way to describe it is with an analogy. In the movie *Saving Private Ryan*, Captain John Miller leads a group of soldiers who have been sent to find Private James Francis Ryan. Ryan is part of a platoon holding a vital bridge in the countryside during the Allied invasion at Normandy. This bridge was vital to the Allied forces that were moving up after the landing at Omaha Beach to cross the river into territory held by the German army. The bridge is a critical link, and the balance of the movie revolves around the small band of soldiers and their heroic efforts to hold the bridge so others can eventually cross it to free France.

In a similar way, Jesus himself is the bridge that connects sinful, fallen people like you and me with the love and forgiveness of a gracious and compassionate heavenly Father. Here is how Jesus is a bridge for us: God created each of us for a relationship with him. We need to be in relationship with God and others, and God's dearest desire is to have a loving intimate relationship with us. Yet each of us has become separated from God. We have chosen to live our lives on our own, making our own decisions and choices. This is what the Bible calls "sin"—willful separation from our loving heavenly Father. The consequence of this separation is death. "For the wages of sin is death [eternal separation from God] but the [free] gift of God is eternal life in Christ Jesus our Lord" (Romans 6:23).

We were born to be in relationship with a loving God and to enjoy his fellowship and blessings in our lives, both now and forever. Our sinfulness has caused separation. It's as if the landmass that we are standing on has had an earthquake split open a crevasse as wide as the Grand Canyon between God and us. This is the cost of separation—life without God: a type of living, painful death now, and separation for all of eternity once our physical body dies.

Many have tried to cross the gulf between God and themselves through their own efforts. This is the intent of living a life of good works, being religious, doing things to get close to God, achieving great success and fame, or being philanthropic. All these efforts fall short, and none of us through our own efforts can bridge the Grand Canyon gap between ourselves and God. It's a mile wide! No matter how hard we try, our efforts are simply never going to be enough to create a bridge to reconnect us to God.

Jesus, however, through his sinless life and sacrificial death on the cross, has solved the problem for us. Jesus has created a bridge of love across the gap, which separates us from God. If we put our trust in him, rather than in ourselves and our own efforts, we can be restored into a loving relationship with God. "Yet to all who received him, to those who believed in his name, he gave the right to become the children of God" (John 1:12).

During the Great Depression, police brought an elderly man before a New York City night court magistrate. The man was starving and had stolen a loaf of bread. That night, Mayor Fiorello Laguardia was presiding over the court, as he sometimes did to stay close to the citizens. He fined the old man ten dollars. "The law is the law, and cannot be broken," the mayor said. At the same time, he took a ten dollar bill out of his wallet and paid the fine for the man. Then Laguardia cited each person in the courtroom for living in a city that did not help its poor and elderly, unduly tempting them to steal. The mayor fined everyone in the audience fifty cents and gave almost fifty dollars to the amazed defendant. Both justice and love were served when Laguardia paid the penalty and more for the old man.

Jesus has made a way where there was no way. That is the good news, the gospel. Jesus has created a bridge we can walk over into a life of forgiveness, healing, and restoration as we experience a personal relationship with a gracious, loving, heavenly Father. It is a free gift! But like any gift, we have to decide to reach out and accept it. One of the most powerful elements of God's love for us is that he gives us the right to choose. While he created us and he is the all-powerful sustainer and creator of the universe, he never imposes his will on us—even if it is what is best, what we need, what we want. In his love for us, he leaves us free to choose. We can choose life in him through Jesus. Or we can choose separation—death both now and forever.

> We human beings have been given the terrible gift of free will, and this ability to make choices, to help write our own story, which is what makes us human even when we make the wrong choices… it is the ability to choose which makes us human.[54]

It is simple to do, walking over this bridge. Even a child can do it, it is that easy. It doesn't depend at all on our ability, our maturity, or our worthiness. We don't need to know or understand Scripture. We don't need to attend church. It is a free gift. Jesus says we have to accept the gift like a child. And it's probably easier for a child—they aren't hung up on all sorts of thoughts about their roles in accepting a free gift. Madeleine L'Engle says,

> It may be that we have lost our ability to [accept God's wonderful gift] because we've been taught that such things have to be earned; we should deserve them. We must be qualified. We are suspicious of grace. We are afraid of the very lavishness of the gift. But a child rejoices in presents![55]

You can accept this free gift right now wherever you are. Simply stop and talk to your heavenly Father:

Dear God,

I admit I have sinned and fallen short and that I am separated from you. I want to accept the free gift of life in Jesus. I put my life in your hands and trust you as my savior. Thank you for loving me and for giving me the gift of new life—both now and forever. I pray this in Jesus' name. Amen.

Chapter Fourteen

WALKING IN THE LIGHT

So what happens when you pray this prayer or simply decide in your heart to trust Jesus? The spiritual reality is Jesus comes into your life and begins to help you discover a new life in him. He says,

> "Here I am! I stand at the door and knock. If anyone hears my voice and opens the door, I will come in and eat with him, and he with me" (Revelation 3:20).

> "I am making everything new!... I am the Alpha and the Omega, the Beginning and the End. To [those] who [are] thirsty I will give to drink without cost from the spring of the water of life. [Those] who overcomes will inherit all this, and I will be his God and [they] will be my [children]" (Revelation 21:5-7).

A spiritual transformation has taken place. It seals your relationship with God both now and for eternity. The Holy Spirit comes to live in your life. He is Jesus, ever present in your life to give you the wisdom and spiritual resources to live a new life here on earth. He is also a deposit, a down payment of life to come in eternity. The life we live here on earth is like the tip of an iceberg. What you see is only a small fraction of what is to come. As spiritual beings engaged in the human experience, we often make the mistake of thinking the visible tip is the whole iceberg. The reality of our lives as spiritual beings is so much larger, better, and finer than the visible part we see in this life. We are often misled into a distorted understanding of life. One of the Holy Spirit's jobs is to live within us and teach us to live as spiritual beings created by a loving God.

Let me warn you about the experience that happens after you accept the free gift of Jesus' love. There is almost as much variation in your new spiritual life as there are people who populate the world today. There is no one set experience you should expect. Some people have a tremendous sense of relief as the burden of guilt, pain, and fear is lifted off their shoulders. Others have a quiet, glowing peace that begins to fill and to penetrate all aspects of their lives. Some have a powerful emotional experience—almost a "rush" or a high of spiritual power and cleansing released in their lives. Many others experience no emotion at all.

I felt little or no emotion when I met Jesus. I knew I had taken a step of faith, and I hoped God would begin to do stuff in my life, but for almost a year there was no emotional high or any other supernatural experience. I just found myself talking to God, and trying to walk each day with Jesus while learning about myself, my life, and his love, as I went on with life.

It was like the coming of daylight after a long night. It was pitch black, and had been for a long time. No stars, no light. Gradually, the sky takes on a shadow background of light, but it is hidden behind all the pervasive darkness. Gradually, you have this sense it is getting lighter, but you really can't see anything. This goes on for some time and then suddenly you realize you can see stuff you couldn't see before. It's actually light! But you couldn't say exactly when it came—it just did. It was dark, but now it's light and you can see. You aren't sure how it happened, but you know it's real and you're glad for it. That's what my first year walking with Jesus was like.

When I first got into conversation about Jesus with my friend Moffit, I was obviously at a point of spiritual need. Moffit was aware of the spiritual quest I was engaged in, because of her own searching years. We both realized I was ready to take the step of faith and put my trust and my life into Jesus' hands.

So what happened when I prayed that prayer on the sidewalk on 23rd Street in Ocean City, New Jersey? When I got up, I knew I had been lost in the woods all my life. Now I had broken out of the trees into an open field and in some way was "found." I really had no idea what this meant, but I knew it was coming from my new relationship with Jesus. I knew, as I walked with him, it would eventually get clearer and I would know what to do.

For the next year, the only guidance I had was from talking with God. My prayer relationship with Jesus and the Holy Spirit living in me gave me wisdom and hope and showed me how to deal with the day-to-day issues in my life. I can remember standing by Green Lane Lake in Pennsylvania talking to God while I fished for trout. I remember talking to God while driving down the road on my way to work, or sitting outside having a last cigarette before bed. Somehow, when I talked to Jesus, he spoke to me in my spirit and gave me the love and guidance I needed.

A year later, I was back in Ocean City, and I hooked up with some folks who were friends of Jesus. One of them told me she had met a guy who knew Jesus and told her she could learn more about God by his letters to his followers—the Bible. I went with her and I met this guy. He gave me a copy of the Bible, which I had never actually read. To be honest, I had never tried to read it. The paperback version he gave me *(Good News for Modern Man)* was simple, straightforward, and easy to read.

As I began to pray and read the Bible, more of God's guidance for my life kicked in. Later that fall, I met a guy who invited me to a small meeting of people who were friends of Jesus. This was incredible! Here were people who knew and loved Jesus and were quite mature in their experience and walk with him. This really poured fuel on my fire—to know God and to walk with him each day. Over the next several years, these men opened their lives to me and invested in helping me grow spiritually. With their friendship, I grew to the point where I was able to reach out and help younger believers in their walk with God.

My first reaction to God wasn't very emotional, and I never had what I would call a spiritual high. Even though my first year of growth was pretty rocky, by the end of two or three years, I could look back and see Jesus really had transformed my life for the better. I could look forward with every expectation he would continue the process of keeping the good, tossing out the bad, and bringing in more of his good. During these days I often reflected on Martin Luther King, Jr.'s famous quote, "Lord, I ain't what I wanna be. I ain't what I'm gonna be, but thank God I ain't what I was!"

Stan Telchin was fifty years old, a faithful husband, and a father of two with a successful insurance business in the Washington, DC area. As a Jew, he had no real interest in spiritual things, but through some dramatic changes in his daughter's life (as told in his book *Betrayed*), he began a spiritual quest. After ninety days of searching and reading and talking to others, his faith in Jesus as the Messiah and his Savior came in an instant. Sitting on a stone bench, struggling with his fears and prejudices, he was confronted by God. He said,

> [I] was able to recognize that despite the weeks of counting the cost, the overwhelming truth was greater than the cost. The power of the truth was greater than the

power of fear. An enormous load had been lifted from my heart. Inside of me, a singing began to come forth, a joy I had never experienced before and I reveled in it![56]

My friend Teresa said that when she first trusted Christ, it was a lot like that scene in the *Indiana Jones* movie where he is searching for the Holy Grail.

In the movie *Indiana Jones and the Last Crusade,* Jones has reached at the final part of his search to discover the Holy Grail. Much is at stake for Jones; he needs the Grail's power to save his dying father. He has already faced and succeeded in two of the three challenges that prevent "the unworthy" from getting to the Grail, but now he comes out on the edge of an incredibly deep and wide ravine, its bottom lying out of sight. It is far too wide to jump across, but it is obvious the entrance to the crypt, which holds the Grail, is on the other side of this impassable ravine. According to the legend, this is called "The Path of God."

Jones realizes, through the riddle he is given, that it is only by leaping across this ravine that he can prove he is "worthy" of the Grail. The leap is humanly impossible. But he realizes if he wants to save his father's life, he has to take action. It's a leap of faith. Closing his eyes, he steps out into the empty space and the bottomless pit...

His foot lands on solid rock. He is astonished and relieved. From this new perspective, he can now see there is a stone bridge. It had been perfectly camouflaged; when standing above, it was invisible to the human eye. But now, with his feet on solid ground, he sees the footbridge that can safely enable him to cross to the other side to the place of the Holy Grail.

Teresa told me beginning to walk with Christ was like that—walking out on an invisible bridge and trusting that when she moved forward with Jesus she would be safe; that he would lift her up and hold her and keep her from going too far to the left or to the right and falling into a ravine of oblivion.

"I felt like I had to trust him and at least to try it. So each time I trusted him, I said, "I'm going to try it and if it doesn't work I'll bail out, quit, or back off."

"So I worked up my nerve and tried it. And he was there! He was true! He was reliable! It felt so good I kept doing it more—trusting him again and again. Eventually, I began to trust him for little things in everyday life. It was like that reading the Bible. At the beginning I didn't understand it. But I read it and I trusted him to give me something out of it. And each day he gave me something that I could understand or that I could apply and learn from."

Teresa says during her first weeks walking with God, it was "scary to be a believer out loud. But as I trusted him and obeyed him, I found I got more and more comfortable with it and more assured of his love and his trustworthiness."

Evelyn Lewis Perera's life began to change when her sister Vee started to walk with Jesus. Her sister's growing spiritual health and vitality convinced Evelyn to wrestle with her own inner spiritual condition. After months of searching and struggling, her quest came to resolution. She described what happened and the aftermath in her life:

> I wrestled through the next few days. Occasionally, I would find a verse in the Bible that temporarily quieted the storm inside. Eventually, I centered on one verse, Mark 9:24, presumably recalled from Sunday school. I began to repeat it over and over while folding diapers, "Lord, I believe; help thou my unbelief." Not long afterwards—I woke up in the middle of the night—and I knew that I believed in the risen Christ.

It would make a conveniently resolved story if everything in my life changed the same night. But even though I had acknowledged Jesus Christ I was still too proud to repent of all I knew I should repent of. I still had a good dose of "the self yeast of the spirit." In fact, I had a nervous breakdown and spent time in a mental hospital. But spirit and mind are closely intertwined. Looking back on my childhood I realized painful experiences and unwise actions played a role in the later onset of mental darkness and thereby solidified my will's resistance to retraining.

Yet all things worked together for good for those who love God. I see now that this episode was integral to the long process of healing and renewal that my loving Creator began in me when I used that verse from Mark's gospel to pray for faith. What seemed like a period of disorder was part of a necessary restructuring of the self, the process of inner purging... as I opened my life to God and began to dismantle and reorganize, he began to substitute his quality of life—joy, kindness, and patience—for a life of fear, pride, and faithlessness.[57]

Let me talk to you for a moment about that term "believer." To be a believer does not mean you have arrived. Typically, it is used to refer to someone who has made a commitment to Jesus, has accepted his free gift of new life and is walking towards God. That's how Jesus used the term when he said, "For God so loved the world that he gave his one and only Son, that whoever believes in him shall not perish but have eternal life" (John 3:16).

To be a believer, however, does not mean a person has arrived, made the grade, or is in any way better than you and me. People who are believers are broken, hurting, sinful people whose lives are still pretty messed up. But they are saved by grace. They are in the process of moving toward God and having his light and love shine in their lives, changing them for the better.

When Jesus was being hung on the cross, there were two common thieves who were being crucified with him. One cried out to Jesus, "Jesus, remember me when you come into your kingdom." Jesus answered him, "I tell you the truth, today you will be with me in paradise" (Luke 23:42-43). The thief "believed," although it should be clear he hadn't time to develop a detailed theology. What did he believe in? He believed in Jesus. It should also be clear the thief didn't have time to clean up the elements of his life which had led to his criminal execution. He simply put his faith in Jesus and that was enough.

Being a believer is a process that operates at three levels. To simply turn toward God and to seek him makes you a believer. God promises as we seek him, he will find us. As we seek a personal relationship, he will speak to our hearts in a language we can understand and will help us get back into relationship with him. All we have to do is start. God is committed to helping each of us get there.

The second level of being a believer is when you meet Jesus and put your trust in him. This also is more about what Jesus does for you than what you do as a believer. Like the thief on the cross, Jesus does all the work and we get all the benefits. We are forgiven, we are given grace, we are given a fresh start at life, and we are given all of God's spiritual resources when we put our trust in Jesus.

Finally, there is a third level at which we can become believers. That is when we get up every morning and decide we are going to follow Jesus *today*. The way you live your life tells us what you really believe. It's not about what you say or think. It's about the decisions and choices you make to seek God, to walk with Jesus, and to respond to the gentle urging of the Holy Spirit each day. Believing is something we do in our hearts. No one else can judge from the outside what we truly believe. As God said to one of the prophets, "Man looks at the outward appearance, but the Lord looks at the heart" (1 Samuel 16:7).

When you first reach out and put your hand in Jesus' hand, you begin a journey. No matter how it feels at the moment, a new life has begun. You will never be the same. Jesus will take the good things in your life and build on them; he will transform them into better versions of what you already had. He will begin to take the difficult, troubling things in your life and heal them. Some he can cure over time, others he will cut out and dispose of. He will begin to bring new things into your life—wonderful things which will give you immense joy and satisfaction in your living today and forever.

Chapter Fifteen

QUESTIONS AND DOUBTS

When considering the possibility of a personal relationship with God, we often find ourselves asking a variety of questions. Many are concerns we have long entertained, issues which make us hesitant to get closer to God. Nagging doubts make us question if God can be loving. Or make us fear that getting close to God may require us to turn off our brains, forget our questions, or simply take the fun from our life.

I certainly don't claim to have all the answers, but I do know from my own experience and from the experience of others, that God welcomes our questions, doubts, and fears. At some point, it is true, we have to take a step of faith to move forward into a relationship with God. But he always welcomes us with our doubts and questions. He wants us to use our minds, our hearts, and our emotions to seek out the truth about him and his love.

God is a God of light and truth. The closer you move toward him and into the light, the more you will find he will speak to your questions and concerns in a language you can understand. So while I cannot promise to provide the specific answers you need (only Jesus can do that), I would be happy to share with you what I've learned from my own struggle with some of the most common questions seekers have.

How can a God who allows suffering and evil be good and kind?

The problem of human suffering and evil in the world is universal. There is no one who will read this book who in someway has not been touched by suffering, pain, loss, and evil inflicted upon innocent victims. If not in your own life, then you have experienced it vicariously through others you love or care about. While large-scale suffering in the world often claims the attention of the media, I think it is the personal tragedies which most often move us to compassion.

Cynthia J. Brennan, age thirty-eight, a cocktail waitress earning $30,000 a year, fed some coins in a slot machine at the Las Vegas Desert Inn on January 27, 2000, and won $34,959,458—the largest slot pay out in history. She promptly quit her job, married her boyfriend, and set up a trust fund to help out the members of her family with her newfound riches. Less than six weeks later, she was rear-ended by an unlicensed, drunk driver while stopped at an intersection. Her older sister, Lela, was killed in the accident. Cindy's fifth vertebra was smashed, her spinal cord severed. Now bound to a wheel chair with no hope she will ever walk again, she says, "You can be on top of the world one minute and all of a sudden you are paralyzed."[58]

Madeleine L'Engle tells this horrible story about a good Christian family:

> One afternoon the mother is giving her baby a bath. The doorbell downstairs rings, shrilly, urgently. She rushes to answer it. Her older child follows her, trips, falls down the stairs, and breaks his neck. She opens the door to be told her husband has just been killed at an accident at work. Upstairs the baby drowns in the tub. How can we react to such horrors except, "to curse God and die"?[59]

Human pain and suffering are all too evident in our world. We could fill several books with examples, but most of us can come up with our own.

There are two primary reasons we experience a world filled with suffering. The first reason is God, in his grace, allows humans to have free will. God has created the world and created each of us. But it is not a closed system where he makes us do what is right and good for each person. Every one of us has the right to do what is good and loving to others and ourselves, or to do that which is harmful and wrong. God will ultimately hold people accountable for their behavior, but he doesn't protect us from the natural consequences of our actions.

He allows us to create a hammer, which can drive nails and be used to build a house—i.e., to do good. At the same time, if someone chooses to, they can pick up the hammer and hit another over the head killing them. God does not intervene and change the physical properties of the tool so that it becomes a Nerf™ hammer which bounces harmlessly off the victim. To do so, would leave us as mere puppets on the world's stage with God pulling the strings and making us dance to his tune.

God lets us make choices freely, but he also lets us suffer natural consequences. I had a neighbor living near my camp in Maine. This man was well known and well loved in his community. Chuck was a man of faith who loved God. He was constantly serving others, especially the kids in his small rural town.

He died unexpectedly at the age of fifty-three. His wife and adult children were so angry with God for allowing him to die at such a young age. However, they never stopped to consider the large amounts of alcohol Chuck drank which led to cirrhosis of the liver, or the three packs of cigarettes he smoked each day, which produced lung cancer. They never acknowledged his personal choices might have contributed to his early demise. Perhaps it wasn't God's will at all, but simply the consequences of Chuck's behavior.

The tragic traffic accident, which left Cindy J. Brennan paralyzed and her sister dead, wasn't exactly an act of God. The driver who hit her, Clark Morse, fifty-eight, was heading home from a bar and was going 50 miles per hour into the intersection when he rear-ended Cindy Brennan and her sister. Morse had previously been arrested fifteen times for drunk driving, had a blood-alcohol level twice the legal limit allowed by Nevada law, was driving his mother's car without permission, and had lost his driver's license due to previous drunk driving convictions.

> The problem of pain, war and the horror of war, of poverty, and disease is always confronting us, but a God who allows no pain, no grief, also allows no choice. There is little unfairness in a colony of ants, but there is also little freedom. We human beings have been given the terrible gift of free will, and this ability to make choices, to help write our own story, is what makes us human, even if we make the wrong choices, abusing our freedom and the freedom of others. The weary and war torn world around us bears witness to the wrongness of many of our choices. George McDonald gives me renewed strength during times of trouble—times when I've seen people tempted to deny God—when he said, "The son of God suffered onto death, not that men might not suffer, but that their sufferings might be like his."[60]

The second primary cause of human suffering is that we live in a fallen world. God created the world and created humans to enjoy it. Mankind has rebelled. To this day, a majority of people are living in rebellion against God. The result of the "fall" is that evil and sin has entered the world and permeates the very fabric of our lives. The world we live in is a mixture of good and bad. God is actively involved in our world. He brings good and blessing to everyone—regardless of their relationship with him. He allows the sun and the rain to fall on the just and the unjust. Crops grow; progress produces further comfort for humans, and many good things flow to all who populate the world.

At the same time, evil and injustice also permeate the fabric of our lives. The rich oppress the poor; nations go to war or persecute minorities; sexual sin causes AIDS and other diseases; human sin causes all kinds of pollution, injustice, damage, and harm to innocent humans in the same world. Jesus said, "God's world is like a field where good wheat seed has been planted [by God], but the enemy came out at night and sowed weed seeds in the midst of the good seed." Rather than pull the weeds now, Jesus says God will pull the weeds and burn them when the crop is ripe and ready for harvest. This is so the good won't be destroyed by the attempt to root out the bad (Matthew 13).

Heaven is simply the world we are headed toward where all the bad has been removed. Rather than the mix of good and bad, which we now experience, it is totally, 100 percent, the good that flows from God's presence, his personality, and his love. Hell isn't some fiendish torture chamber; it is simply a place where all the mitigating good of God's presence has been removed. It is life for eternity without God's presence. It is 100 percent evil, full of pain, suffering, and torment—not because of some plan of God's, but simply as a result of the absence of God.

Why would a loving God condemn anyone to an eternity in Hell?

He wouldn't, he hasn't, and he won't. Yet at the same time, God chooses not to violate the free will he has given to people as part of their creation. What is God's will for every person?

"Your Father in heaven is not willing that any of these little ones should be lost" (Matthew 18:14).

"For God so loved the world that he gave his one and only Son, that whoever believes in him shall not perish but have eternal life. For God did not send his Son into the world to condemn the world, but to save the world through him" (John 3:16-17).

The Lord is not slow in keeping his promise, as some understand slowness. He is patient with you, not wanting anyone to perish, but everyone to come to repentance (2 Peter 3:9).

God's desire is for everyone to join his family and to spend eternity with him, but his love for us is so great he simply will not force people to accept his love against their will.

A college friend of my daughter's helped create this word picture to explain God's respect for us. "If God was a big guy, say three stories tall (about 30 feet), and he approached me (Martha is about 5 feet tall and 105 pounds soaking wet) to convince me to do his will, he could obviously force me to do anything he wanted. He could pick me up by the scruff of the neck with his finger and thumb and make me do whatever he wanted. But my compliance, my obedience wouldn't be love and it wouldn't be freely given."

God is so much bigger and more powerful than we are, yet he still respects us and lets us choose. We can choose to love him or not. We can choose to respond to his love in Jesus or not. We can disobey him or obey him as we wish. He will never make us do his will, even if it is best for us.

And that is the point. God lets us choose. We can choose to respond to him and walk with him, both in this life and for eternity (that's heaven). Or we can rebuff his attempts to reach out to us and close our hearts to him and spend all of eternity outside of his presence (that's hell).

Exploring God Without Getting Religious

Can I have faith in something I cannot see?

How to put your faith in a person you can't see remains a mystery for many people. Our culture, based on scientific rationalism, reinforces a worldview which says, "If I cannot see it or touch it or test it with a repeatable experiment, then how can it be real?"

Yet our own experience shows this worldview, as prevalent as it is in the beginning of the 21st century, cannot possibly be true. The wind is real, but I cannot see it. When it turns into storms, tornadoes, and hurricanes, it becomes immensely powerful; I can see the result of its action, but I still can't see it. Splitting an atom releases enough force to destroy entire cities, or conversely, to heat and power all the homes in a city. I can't see it or touch it, but I take it on faith that it is real. Love between one person and another cannot be tested or run through a series of experiments, but you can literally see it happen between two people. How and why does it happen? I don't know. It is a mystery.

My friend Teresa had her first granddaughter born yesterday. Last night she chatted on and on, and bubbled happily about this six-pound bundle of life: her personality, her gifts, her abilities, and so on.

Now I was thinking this child sounded like any other undefined, red, wrinkled, baby, but to her grandmother—the love affair of a lifetime had been launched. Nothing in this world or the next would ever be able to quench her flames of adoration for this child. Is it empirical, factual, and testable? No, but it is *real* and *powerful*.

Madeleine L'Engle makes an interesting statement about the faith of atheists, people who hold a strong conviction that there is no God:

> Atheism is a peculiar state of mind: you cannot deny the existence of that which does not exist. I cannot say,

"that chair is not there" if there is no chair there to say it about. Many atheists deny God because they care so passionately about a caring and personal God and the world around them is inconsistent with a God of love, they feel, and so they say "there is no God."[61]

One of my wife's friends is a woman who cares deeply and passionately about life and people, but says she is an atheist. Upon closer examination, I found she had a childhood that failed to meet her expectations. Her mother was a demanding and controlling woman.

Her husband was stricken with leukemia during the prime of life and died within five months of first discovering the disease. This friend has been left with two adolescent children to finish raising, and life is not working out the way she hoped.

Her conclusion: "How can there be a God? There is no one controlling the world, my life, and the people in my life to produce the outcome I envisioned. So God cannot exist. If he did, he would have given me what I wanted from life!"

Many years ago, A wise Old Testament scholar, Dr. Marvin Wilson, gave me some advice on understanding faith and God's ways. He said, "Understanding God's ways is like having a house with thirteen windows and eleven screens. No matter how you arrange them, there are always going to be some holes you can't cover."

His point is well taken. As finite human creatures, we have a limited ability to truly understand a God who is unlimited, all-powerful and wise, and loving beyond compare. God's ways are often too big for us to fathom with our weak and fallible intellects. Many issues do come down to simple faith. Dr. Wilson told me, "Whenever your theology (man's understanding of how God works) and your experience of God disagree, throw out your theology." Some might consider Wilson's comment heretical, but it makes a lot of sense. Our theology or our understanding of God will always be limited and defective because of our human limitations and sin. God's love for us is constant and never changing. You are safe in the loving arms of Jesus.

If God is so loving, why am I in so much pain?

Sometimes people voice this concern in a slightly different way. "How come bad things happen to good people?" But the real question for each of us is usually personal. "I am in real pain—so why isn't God doing something to solve, remove, or take the pain out of my life?"

Brent Foster describes his high school years growing up in Iowa as a series of unbroken successes. His peers described him as a bright person with a bright future. He was elected President of almost every major organization in school, and his academic success was recognized statewide. He became famous for playing high school basketball on an artificial leg. His years of success culminated in becoming class valedictorian and gaining a coveted seat in the freshman class of Harvard University. Foster writes,

> Now here I am, an accomplished Harvard student, the world seemingly at my feet. However there is one little catch to all of this success: I have wide spreading bone cancer and only several weeks to live. These were supposed to have been the best years of my life, instead I am at the losing end of an eight-year battle with cancer. And although only 21, my body has grown extremely weak and will soon fail me altogether. In fact, every breath in itself has become a struggle. After a total of 11 surgeries, a year of chemotherapy, and a month of high dose radiation, the doctors can do nothing more. From my experiences I have wondered if humans were created with more capacity for pain than happiness.[62]

When we are honest with ourselves, we realize we really believe the purpose of life is to grant us a large measure of personal

Questions and Doubts

prosperity and peace. It's what we really want for ourselves and for those we love and care about. Many of us feel, if God was any good at his job, we wouldn't be enduring pain and suffering; and better yet, our lives would be rich with blessings.

C.S. Lewis, in his book *A Grief Observed*, states that God doesn't promise us freedom from adversity and pain. Lewis says that the Bible is clear that there is pain and suffering in our world because of us—because *we* rebelled against the laws of God. He goes on to say that we can still rejoice, however. We have been given the spiritual resources we need, through Christ, to overcome.

> In *A Grief Observed*, C.S. Lewis wrote about his reactions to the loss of his wife—the one person who was to him everything worthwhile on this earth. The book is a magnificent document for a psychiatrist to read, for it expresses with remarkable clarity the process of mourning and grief. Lewis makes you feel it. He describes the anger, the resentment, loneliness, and fear fluttering in the stomach and restlessness—how the world seemed dull and flat—how he could find no joy in his work. Could God in the final analysis, he wondered, be a cruel God? Was God, ultimately, a cosmic sadist? In the agony of his grief, he tried to pray. Though his need was desperate, he sensed only a door slammed in his face and the sound of bolting and double bolting from inside.
>
> He felt that God had forsaken him. There was only the locked door, the iron curtain, the vacuum, absolute zero. He soon realized that in his desperation he was not knocking at the door; he was trying to kick it down. Then slowly, gradually, like the dawning of a clear spring day, with the light and warmth of the sun, his faith began to bolster him; to give him renewed strength, comfort, and

what he describes as "unspeakable joy". He knocked—and this time the door was opened. He experienced again the presence of him upon whom his hope was based.[63]

In my own experience of pain and suffering, I have learned a few truths over the years. Pain can actually serve a constructive purpose in our life—it can help us to grow. Don't get me wrong—I don't pray, "Give me the pain, Lord, so that I can feel the gain." Not a chance! Yet my own bouts with very painful experiences show God has taken these painful experiences and transformed me into a deeper, richer, more compassionate, more sympathetic person as a result of having walked through a period of suffering.

It is much like the body's own physical health. Pain in our body is a way of nurturing health. If you get a splinter or a cut and it gets infected, eventually the increasing spread of pain will cause you to seek medical attention before you get gangrene and lose a limb. When you get a toothache, you go to the dentist so you can get medical attention before the rot can spread into your system and destroy your jaw. Leprosy is a disease that robs a person of pain. Due to a bacterial infection in the nerve endings, the patient eventually loses any sensation in the extremities. This inability to feel pain leads to all kinds of infections, wounds, and damage; which eventually deform and erode the flesh in these areas.

I dated a girl in high school whose mother was married to a doctor. As I got to know the family, I found out the doctor was Katie's stepfather and that he was an alcoholic. Then I discovered the doctor regularly came home and beat Katie's mom and would chase her around the house while firing live rounds at her from his .357 Magnum pistol trying to kill her. If that wasn't astonishing enough, I later found out this was actually the mom's third husband. The previous two husbands were also alcoholic doctors who came home and smacked her around the house and tried to shoot her with their handguns. As much as I felt tremendous sympathy for Katie and her mother's awful predicament, even more, I wondered what would cause a woman to keep marrying man after man who would treat her like this? Didn't the pain cause her to stop and re-evaluate her choices and their consequences?

While God never causes bad or painful things to happen to us, he can use them to restore us to health. As Madeleine L'Engle says,

> Jesus came into the world to save sinners, to look for the lost sheep, to heal the blind, deaf, and dumb, and lepers and those possessed by demons to give hope to the wounded and bleeding and broken. Jesus came to fulfill the prophecy and go to the cross and break the barriers of time and space in the mighty act of at-one-ment with all of creation.
>
> God does not promise us protection anymore than he promised it to Jesus or Jacob. We are not given protection. We are given vulnerability. We are promised not the absence of pain, but the blessed warning of pain. We are promised not that we won't be wounded, that we won't bleed, but that we will be transfused. We are promised not that we won't die, but that we shall live.[64]

Bearing pain and suffering through difficult circumstances is always a hard experience. I don't think there are any easy, pat answers to give to a person who is facing any of the terrible and contradictory things that afflict us in this broken world. Yet Jesus shares our suffering. He, too, was afflicted with incredible suffering and pain. An innocent and sinless man, he was executed by having nails driven into his wrists and ankles and hanging from a cross with his life ebbing away over many hours until he was dead. Whatever pain you or a loved one is going through, Jesus has been there and he will suffer with you through your pain.

Brent Foster shares of the comfort he received from knowing of Christ's love and suffering as he faced his own death from bone cancer:

> Mere words are meaningless, especially in the face of death. At such times as these, the only respite for me is to "remember my Creator." For in Christ there is a meaning deeper than our understanding and ability to formulate into human speech. As Paul so correctly wrote in 1 Cor. 4:20: "The Kingdom of God is not a matter of talk but of power."
>
> God himself suffered much more than even I can imagine when he became a man, and can, therefore, understand our deepest sorrows. I am always moved when I read the account of Jesus visiting the tomb of Lazarus. When seeing the considerable grief that death had inflicted on his people, Jesus himself wept. Even though he would soon revive Lazarus, Jesus was overcome with sorrow that humanity had been reduced to such a state and consequently forced to endure such pain. I've always placed my hope in the promise that, just as Christ revived Lazarus, he will come and fix our brokenness also. It is easy to forget this compassion of Christ, even though he actually chose to save mankind by subjecting himself to suffering. There is a mystery in God's use of suffering to bring renewal and redemption which I don't completely understand."[65]

So if you find yourself in a painful period in your life, don't give up hope and don't write off God. He is a God of love who does not stand aside and look on suffering unmoved. God is part of your suffering, and he wants you to have Jesus and all of his spiritual resources to give you the strength to bear things we do not think we could possibly bear. And because he is with us in our suffering, our spirit and person are helped to grow stronger and better and to reach full maturity—if not in this life, then in life with him for eternity. As Madeleine L'Engle says, "God does not want or cause bad things to happen. But with God's patient and unfailing love, they can be redeemed."[66]

Why doesn't God answer my prayers?

A dear friend of mine is single and would really love to be married. I met her when she was forty, and at that time she had been divorced for about nine years. Her first husband abandoned her, causing much pain and damage to her self-esteem. She has an active faith and has been friends with Jesus for many years. She wonders how God could have allowed her to make the mistake of marrying her first husband. She has now been single for fourteen years and feels she has worked through all the issues she had contributed to her failed marriage. She loves people, is very extroverted, and longs for the companionship of a good husband. So why hasn't God answered her prayers and connected her to an appropriate guy? To be truthful, I don't know.

Another friend got married for the first time in his mid-thirties. He and his wife really wanted to settle down and raise a big family. After their first daughter was born, they were thrilled. They anticipated having several more children.

Soon she conceived, but after carrying the baby for only five months, the child aborted from undiagnosed internal complications. After a year of rest, grieving, and recovery, my friend's wife discovered, much to their delight, she was again pregnant. We prayed hard for the delivery of a healthy baby. I prayed, my wife prayed, my friends prayed, and many others prayed as well. After about six months, however, this child was also lost under similar circumstances. Why weren't our prayers answered? Again, I don't know.

Dan was an extremely bright and capable guy who began his career working in the healthcare industry. After holding a number of increasingly responsible management positions leading to a vice presidency, he resigned and went to seminary to study God's views on the workplace. After graduation, Dan created a new organization, specifically designed to minister God's grace and love to people in the marketplace. This young organization took off and became a major influence in the Boston metro area. Several years into this project, Dan was diagnosed with a serious type of liver disease. After waiting for a couple of years, he received a liver transplant. Everyone was excited and relieved. The prognosis of a full recovery and a return to leadership of this highly innovative and influential organization was excellent. But less than twelve months later, at the age of thirty-five, Dan was dead. He left behind a grieving widow and two young children. Hundreds of people were praying for his recovery and return to a healthy and productive life over a period of years. Why didn't God answer their prayers? *I don't know.*

Let me tell you what I do know about prayer. First, I'm sure God hears all of our prayers—yours, mine, and anyone who chooses to address him in word, thought, or deed. God is all present, all knowing, all loving, all powerful. I know it isn't a problem of communicating with him. He isn't off duty; he isn't hard of hearing. He is available 24/7 and is always listening to every one of his children, if they care to talk with him. I know he is able to deal with them all, all the time, although I don't know how. But I know it is true, so it isn't a volume or capacity problem, either. I also know it isn't a problem with our praying "wrong." Scripture says the Holy Spirit can voice our prayer accurately to God even when all we can do is cry out or groan in an inarticulate agony (Romans 8:26).

Another thing I know is God answers our prayers in one of three ways. He can say "yes, "no," "maybe," or "maybe later." One problem is that we tend to interpret "no" or "maybe" as our prayer not being answered. But that is simply not true—God did answer, but he didn't give us the answer we wanted. That's because he is committed to answering our prayers in a way that is *best* for us.

Think of it this way: if my daughter asked me for a few live scorpions to sprinkle on her breakfast cereal just so it would jazz up the plain old "Rice Krispies" (and don't laugh, she's the kind who would), should I answer "yes"? Certainly not! As a loving father, I want to help my kids out any way I can, but I draw the line at giving them anything I know that will be harmful to them. In his superior wisdom, God often has to turn down our prayers because our request isn't really the best thing for us.

I've been praying to win the Publisher's Clearinghouse Sweepstakes for years, but God hasn't answered my prayer (answered it "yes," that is). But given my management of money so far in my life, it may not be a good idea to hand me ten million dollars. It could ruin my life. If you look at the long-term history of many lottery winners, you find winning is often the worst thing that has ever happened to them. So maybe God *is* answering my prayers—he's saying "no."

Sometimes it is an issue of timing. My wife Martie had to wait until she was almost twenty-seven to get married. Her mom used to ask her when she would marry, for all her friends were already married. Of course, by the time Martie found me and we got hitched, a lot of her friends were already getting divorced. After twenty-six years of happy, successful marriage, waiting a little longer for the right guy doesn't seem like such a bad answer to prayer.

At times God answers our prayers, but the answer comes in a different form than we expected, and we might not even recognize it as the answer to the prayer we prayed.

Madeleine L'Engle shares the story of an old man who lived by a river. In the spring, the rains were heavy and the river rose. The

Sheriff came by in his jeep, and said to the old man, "The river is going to flood, and I want to evacuate you." The old man folded his arms confidently. "I have faith in God. God will take care of me." As the water continued to rise, the Sheriff returned in a rowboat and finally a helicopter. The old man refused all efforts to help and finally was drowned in the flood. In heaven, he was very upset. He asked God why he hadn't saved him. God said, "You ninny! I sent you a jeep, a rowboat, and a helicopter!"[67]

God also answers our prayers according to his will. Scripture is clear God wants us to learn to talk to him and communicate frequently. He wants to hear what we are feeling, what we are anxious about, and he wants to know both what we need and desire. The Bible teaches God really wants to say "yes," but this especially applies to prayers in keeping with his will (John 14:13-14; John 16:24).

When my wife and I got married twenty-six years ago, it was the marriage of two very independent, strong willed, and dominant personalities. Both of us are leaders and had learned to exercise our leadership gifts before we got joined at the altar.

The adjustment pains in the first year of marriage were just horrific. We were two immovable titans that needed to be cooperative. We required a great deal of retraining to be able to yield to each other and to be supportive. So difficult was our first year, I began to pray, "God, would you please be so kind and knock off my wife?" I knew how God felt about divorce, so I was convinced it was not an option. So the only other "out" I could think of was that maybe the commuter bus she rode into Boston could accidentally flatten her. Or a piano mover could "Oops!" slip the line, and the ten-story piano freefall could solve all of my problems!

Now I'm glad God didn't answer my prayer. If I understood how he answered prayer, I would have known at the time he wouldn't say "yes." My request was clearly not in keeping with his will—not for my dear wife, nor for our eventually successful relationship.

Why do some think Jesus is the only way?

In our day of pluralism and tolerance of diversity, followers of Jesus often have a reputation for being narrow-minded or intolerant. Sometimes it's deserved, but often it's because of their stated belief that Jesus is the only way to get into a "right" relationship with God. Why would people choose to believe such a narrow-minded thing?

Probably the major reason is because of Jesus' own words about himself. He told his followers, "I am the way and the truth and the life. No one comes to the Father except through me.... Anyone who has seen me has seen the Father." On the same occasion he said, "Believe me when I say that I am in the Father and the Father is in me." At other times he told them, "I am the bread of life. He who comes to me will never go hungry, and he who believes in me will never be thirsty." He said, "I am the light of the world. Whoever follows me will never walk in darkness, but will have the light of life." Finally, he told them, "I am the resurrection and the life. He who believes in me will live, even though he dies; and whoever lives and believes in me will never die" (John 14:6-9; John 14:11; John 6:35; John 8:12; John 11:25-26).

These are pretty incredible claims. Not only does Jesus claim to be the only way to God and to eternal life, he claims to be one with God himself. If you've seen him, you've seen God! No other religious figure in the history of the world has made claims anything like these. C.S. Lewis, a full professor at Oxford University, said you really need to consider the impact of these astounding claims that Jesus makes:

> A man who was merely a man and said the sort of things that Jesus said would not be a great moral teacher... either this man was and is the Son of God, or else a madman or

something worse. You can shut him up for a fool, you can spit at him and kill him as a demon or you can fall at his feet and call him Lord and God. But let us not come with any patronizing nonsense about his being a great human teacher. He has not left that open to us. He did not intend to.[68]

Popular culture would have us believe all religions are equally valid. "Don't all religions lead to God?" is the view of the typical secular person today. This notion is based on our wishful thinking that whatever anyone feels is fine, as long as it doesn't tread on our toes, of course. What poppycock! Certainly no other religious figure in history makes the claims that Jesus does. If Jesus' claims are true, if the Bible is true, then the speculative thinking of other religions can't be true. Jesus says the only way to God and salvation is through faith in him; it is by the free gift of grace alone, not through any effort of our own. The Muslim is told that if he dies murdering infidel Americans or if he is slain in battle in a jihad (holy war) then he is assured a place in heaven with God. These two contradictory views cannot both be right. There is the additional testimony of rational thinking. Do all religions lead to God? Well, let's consider, when I leave the theater at night and I ask for directions to find my way home, what would I think if I was told, "Choose any road; they all lead to your home!" I know what could happen. I could choose one road and end up at the Atlantic Ocean in Eastpoint, Maine; another road would take me to Key West, Florida, before it ran out; a third road would take me to Quebec City, Canada; and a fourth road would leave me stranded on the shores of Lake Michigan in Gary, Indiana. But *none* of these roads would take me home!

In reality, all but a few specific choices of roads will ever have the potential to get me home. Most take me to places I don't want to go. This same principle is true when applied to the notion that all religions lead to God.

Sometimes when people ask this question, what they are really asking is, "What happens to the person in India or Borneo who never hears about Jesus? Does he/she get left out? Is that fair?"

Actually, Scripture gives us some light on that issue. Scripture shows that God is both compassionate and loving, as well as just and fair. Jesus is the fullest expression of God, revealing himself to us so that we can respond to his love.

But God does allow a range of ways through faith to find a relationship with him. His Word says even if you have never heard of Jesus, God reveals enough of himself through nature that a person can trust him and walk toward his light in life. Scripture also tells us that God reveals himself through a person's conscience, so someone who has never heard of Jesus could still respond to him. Each of these involves putting your trust in God and seeking him, accepting the free gift of new life in him.

God wants all of his children back in relationship with him. He is fair, just, and compassionate. Jesus' sacrifice and death on the cross even pays the price for all those in history before his actual death (33 A.D.) who have faith in God. I don't know how. It's a mystery of God I am willing to accept. But the real question is not, "What about the person who has not heard of Jesus?" The real question is, "What are you going to do about Jesus?" You have heard about him; you now know about his offer of grace, so what are you going to do about it?

Here's my suggestion. Give Jesus a try. See if he is there for you. You really have nothing to lose by taking an experimental approach. Try him at his word and see if he won't connect you into a loving relationship with God. He tells you to ask, seek, and knock. If you do, he promises to give, find, and open up to you (Matthew 7:7-8). Ask him to show you if he is the way, the truth, and the life, as well as the only way to the Father. You have everything to gain and nothing to lose, so give him a try!

Chapter Sixteen

TALKING WITH GOD

If you were single and wanted to get married, how would you go about finding a good prospect for a successful relationship? One strategy I've heard described would involve driving to the nearest shopping mall, and taking a few loops around the concourse to check out the people who were there that evening. Then you walk up to the first attractive person you see of the opposite sex and you ask them, "Are you married?" If they reply, "No," then you ask, "Will you marry me?"

This may seem like an outlandish strategy to launch a successful relationship, but in the "relationally-challenged" day and age we live in, many people have lost, or simply never had, the skills to build a relationship.

They resort to all sorts of silly schemes to try and connect with others. Many people find their friendships watching "Oprah" or "Judge Judy" on TV. True, their friendships don't last very long, and there isn't much dialog, but hey, you gotta do what you gotta do. Others spend hours on the Internet and go into chat rooms trying to get to know people. That is another way to build relationships, and it is safe and there is less fear of rejection and catching contagious diseases. Of course, most of what many of these people tell you about themselves isn't true. Maybe some of what you tell them about yourself isn't true either.

So how do you build a good relationship with God in this relationally-starved age? This issue is critical if we are to end up in a personal relationship with a living God, rather than in a religious trap which turns into a dead end. We need to be able to talk with God and to listen to him if we are going to get into a positive and growing relationship. Shortcuts won't work when searching for a mate. There is no easy one-step, drive-thru, quickie trip to the mall to find a good marriage. Nor is there an "easy in-easy out" way to get to know God. We need to plug into our relationship with Jesus, learn to share ourselves, hear from him, draw spiritual resources from him, and let him guide and lead us in life.

We need to recognize that for many of us, prayer will be an unnatural activity. For years and years, we have learned to be self-sufficient, to act on our own, and to call the shots as we see them. The habits of self-reliance, built up over a lifetime, will not melt away in a hurry. Talking to God, telling him how we feel, asking for his help and guidance may be difficult at first. For some, it is an affront to our pride. It seems to be a threat to our habit of independent living.

Even though it may feel unnatural at first, realize that our most intimate relationship with God can only grow as we learn to listen to him and share our lives back with him. It is the key to opening the door to a dialogue which will yield some of the answers you are looking for. It is the way we turn over our fears, anxieties, and experience his peace in our lives. It is the way we hand over our sins, and receive his gift of forgiveness and a fresh start. It is the way he leads us to a new understanding of who we are and how much he loves us, as well as the wonderful things he has waiting for us in our new life in Jesus.

Eventually, it'll dawn on us—we need his help! For Emily Elliott, this need dawned on her slowly. She was raised a Roman Catholic but had always been a reserved, private person. She began to become friends with Jesus when she was invited to join a small group of teachers who met after school. This group would share about their lives, study the Bible, and would pray. For two years Emily participated, but never joined in the prayer part. Finally, she shared, "Even though I never say anything in these meetings, I want you to know God has been working in my life and my trust in him is growing."

Several weeks later during summer vacation, lightning from a late afternoon thunderstorm struck Emily's home and burned it to the ground. She and her family were on vacation when they heard about it. She got home in time to see the firemen putting out the last smoldering embers of what had been her home. We were terrified, thinking this tragedy might have a negative impact on Emily's faith.

But how we underestimate God! Emily's initial reaction was an outpouring of heartfelt thanks to the local firemen. She went around and thanked each one for coming to her family's aid. As she and Kevin surveyed the ruins of the antique colonial they had spent twenty-five years restoring, she thanked God they had been gone when the lightning hit. The bolt hit the room where one of her sons had been doing his summer reading each afternoon. Had they been home, not only the bed and the room, but her son would have been destroyed. She was grateful to God they only lost a house. In short, this tragedy became an opportunity for Emily's faith to grow and mature.

If you haven't yet experienced one of life's unexpected worldrockers, get prepared. You most likely will. If you build your relationship with God before the storms of life hit, you will have a much better chance of surviving them and coming out a stronger person. My observation is these unexpected earthquakes of circumstance have the affect of making a person *bitter* or *better*. Build your relationship with God now, and you will greatly improve your chances of riding out the storms of your lifetime, rather than being pummeled or even destroyed by them.

Talking With God

Brad and Misty Bernall got up on the morning of April 20, 1999, to a day which started out like any other school day in a house with two teenagers. At 7:20 A.M. their two kids, Chris, age fifteen, and Cassie, age seventeen, collected their lunches, said goodbye, and left the house.

Cassie would never return. Hours later she was one of the twelve students gunned down in the shooting at Columbine High School in Littleton, Colorado. In her book about the experience, *She Said Yes,* Misty shares how her relationship with Jesus sustained her through the tragedy and helped her to rise above the overwhelming feelings of anger, revenge, and bitterness. She and her husband have grown into national leaders of a movement dedicated to reaching out to alienated, hostile teens to help them in order to prevent future tragedies. Their relationship with Jesus enabled them to find goodness, mercy, and new hope out of the black hole of loss and despair. Your growing relationship with God can help you find the same when storms overwhelm your life. Learning to talk to God and to hear his voice can help you cope with the fears, anxieties, and circumstances of your life. In God's Word we read,

> Do not be anxious about anything, but in everything, by prayer and petition, with thanksgiving, present your requests to God. And the peace of God, which transcends all understanding, will guard your hearts and your minds in Christ Jesus (Philippians 4:6-7).

That is a promise of God I claim on a daily basis. I have lots of fears, things that cause me anxiety and worry, so I turn them over to him, and he not only takes care of the things I can only worry about, but he replaces my fears and worries with his peace. A great deal! Almost daily we are confronted by decisions we need to make. Sometimes large, sometimes small, but all of them have the potential to cause immediate stress and long-term consequences. God knows this and he offers to help. His Word says, "If any of you lacks wisdom, he should ask God, who gives generously to all without finding fault, and it will be given to him" (James 1:5).

God recognizes our needs and desires to help out. Jesus said,

> "Ask and it will be given to you; seek and you will find; knock and the door will be opened to you. For everyone who asks receives; he who seeks finds; and to him who knocks, the door will be opened" (Matthew 7:7-8).

God is a generous and giving God. Just as we delight in giving our children good things, he delights in giving us wonderful things. "He who did not spare his own Son, but gave him up for us all—how will he not also, along with him, graciously give us all things?" (Romans 8:32). Ask God for the things you need in life. He delights in giving and in generous giving.

One of my daughters, who is a senior in high school, announced she was too grown up and not going on the family vacation during spring break this year. She wanted to stay home and hang out with her friends. After all, she was going away to college soon and this would be her last time to hang out with them. The more we thought about this possibility, the less comfortable we grew. Given some of the choices she had been making, we were definitely worried. Yet we didn't want to force her into rebellion by simply saying, "No!"

So we started to pray. We asked God to come up with an alternative that would be better for her. Last Thursday she went to the dentist for her six-month checkup and cleaning. The dental hygienist, a divorced mother of one of our daughter's girlfriends at school, said, "I was thinking of going on a Caribbean cruise for spring break. It would be so much more fun for Lindsey if she had a friend along. Would you want to come?" Megan was ecstatic! Four days later, the trip was arranged—she'd be spending spring break flying to San Juan and visiting five islands on a cruise liner with Lindsey and her mom. How's that for an answer to prayer?

"God can do anything, you know—far more than anything you can imagine or guess or request in your wildest dreams!" (Ephesians 3:20, *The Message*).

Praying to God is simply having a conversation. You talk out loud or simply in your thoughts. You listen and hear what he has to say. It is just like talking to anyone else. Don't try to use a "special" voice or "special" language. I don't think God is at all impressed with religious language some people use to try impress him. If your four-year old daughter crawled up on your lap and tried to address you as "Oh your most magnificent holiness, great god in the heavens with power who rules on high," how would that make you feel?

Jesus tells us when we talk to God to call him "Abba." That's Aramaic for "Daddy." I had trouble calling God "Daddy" because I never had a close, loving relationship with my earthy father, but that is exactly how God loves us and wants us to relate to him. So relax and be yourself, use your normal tone of voice, speak the words you would use with a friend, and get to know God.

When Jesus taught his followers to pray, he said not to pray to impress others. Your best praying is done in private, so you can be honest and so you hear what God has to say to you. He also said don't babble—just be honest about how you feel, what you think, and where you're at. Don't worry; God is big enough to handle the truth from you! Don't worry about being able to pray well. God already knows what you need, but he does want to connect with you. When you pray, focus on who God is and what he is trying to accomplish in the world. Recognize your own daily need—for sustenance, for forgiveness, for protection from the temptation to do wrong, and for his help to forgive others like God has forgiven you.

Check out Matthew 6:5-15. It's the best advice that I can give you on prayer.

There is tremendous power in the name of Jesus. When you pray, pray in Jesus' name. My daughter has a friend at college who is just beginning to explore who Jesus is and how to have a relationship with God. Karen had a roommate in her sorority who had been a friend of Jesus for some time. They talked a lot about spiritual issues. One night while her roommate was out, Karen had gone to sleep early. She woke up hearing voices in the room. She said, "There was this red vapor hanging over Kathy's bed. It swooped down at me. I was paralyzed by fear. It was clearly a demon, and it was screaming at me in gibberish. I was terrified. As it kept flying at me, I remembered a conversation I had with Kathy, so I cried out, 'In the name of Jesus, I command you to stop!' The demon disappeared immediately. I had this feeling there was a very powerful presence for good in the room. This presence reassured me and calmed me down. It was as if this benevolent spirit was saying, 'You are safe now. It's okay to sleep.'" The name of Jesus is very powerful. When in doubt, just cry out, "Jesus! Help me, Jesus!"

It helps to set a specific time to pray each day, actually praying each day at the same time to develop a habit of praying. I have a regular place I pray in the morning. I do it early before anyone gets up and distracts me. You need to avoid distraction. One friend of mine finds his home so distracting, he goes into the ad agency where he works in Chicago and meets with God before anyone else gets into the office.

I find it also helps me to keep a journal where I write down what I'm thinking or feeling. Sometimes I write down my prayer requests, then I record the answers when God answers them. Other times I'll simply sit with a blank page and I'll listen to the Lord. Then I'll take my pen and write down what he tells me to do.

Some people worry about how to tell if the thoughts popping into their head are from God, rather than their own deluded musings or the result of too many burritos the night before. This is a legitimate concern.

Here's a real eye opener I clipped from a newspaper:

> While working on a contruction job, Thomas W. Passmore, 32, of Norfolk, Virginia, thought he saw the number "666" on his hand. Believing it was a demonic sign, he cut off his hand with a circular saw. He refused to let surgeons reattach his hand, but now he is suing the doctors and the Sentara Norfolk General Hospital for $3.35 million for the loss of his hand.[69]

We aren't left to puzzle this one out on our own: "Is it me, is it God, or is it something else?" God tells us, "the Counselor, the Holy Spirit, whom the Father will send in my name, will teach you all things and will remind you of everything I have said to you" (John 14:26). So ask God himself to clarify if this notion is from him or not.

We are also told to compare what we hear with what we know of Jesus and the Father: is it loving, is it compassionate, is it forgiving, is it healing and helpful to others? Surely the man's decision to cut off his hand would not pass this test.

We are given the whole counsel of the Word of God. The Bible, which we will discuss in the next chapter, is comprised of letters and books written to help believers follow God. We will talk about how to read it and understand it, but regarding prayer, you need to check what you think God is saying to you with what is written in the Bible, and again check it against the big picture of what God says he is like and what he wants us to do. If your prayer leading tells you to quit your job, abandon your wife and kids, and move to Montana to be a naked performance artist, my reading of Scripture would tell me your notion is probably not a thought from God.

Finally, we have the counsel of other believers to help us evaluate the "leadings" we get from prayer. We will talk about the power of community and being in trust relationships with other followers of Jesus in Chapter 18. It is important to bounce your prayer leadings off of other believers, especially those who are more mature and experienced in the faith. God can use them to help confirm or deny the validity of your leading. I'm sure if the man who cut off his hand had checked in with a couple of friends of Jesus, he would still have both hands today.

One last word on prayer. There are several things which can hinder your prayers to God. If you have *unconfessed* sin in your life, it will keep God from answering your prayers or keep you from hearing the answer. If you are cheating on your spouse, you might have to "get right" with God and your spouse before you can expect much success in your prayer life (see 1 John 1:8-10–2:1-2 for more on this topic).

A broken relationship can also impede your relationship with God. Jesus says, "If you are going to worship God and you remember your brother has something against you, leave off your worship. Go at once and make peace with your brother, then come back and offer your worship to God (Matthew 5:23-24).

The last thing which can hinder your prayer life is selfishness. Think about your own experience; if you know a person who only talks about "me," "myself," "I want," and "mine" in your relationship, how interested are you in getting closer to that person? Not very! The same holds true with God. Don't just go to him and babble about all you need and want and how others are unfair to you, and "give me, give me, give me." It is not just about "what's in it for me." You need to go into prayer with an open heart and mind. Tell him how you feel and what you think, but take time to be quiet and to listen. You learn a lot more that way. You will grow much faster in your spiritual life. You will learn more about God's heart of love and learn how to pray more effectively.

Chapter Seventeen

LEARNING FROM GOD

Tom Bowers was a sales manager who worked for me when I lived in Illinois. Tom and his sister Margie had been raised in Liberia where their parents were missionaries. They had both come back to the States to finish high school and attend college. Tom and Margie were very close. He says, "Next to my wife Kathy, Margie was my best friend. That's why it was inconceivable to me when on April 29, 1977, Margie (age twenty-five) was brutally murdered in her apartment in Oak Park, Illinois."

Margie returned to her apartment that evening and was confronted by Thomas Vanda, who was looking for her roommate Esther. When Margie refused to give him any information, he flew into a rage and attacked her with a knife, stabbing her repeatedly. A neighbor heard her dying screams and called the police who captured Vanda.

Tom tells of the agony he struggled through for the next fifteen years—the numbness and denial that followed his sister's death, and the burning anger and desire to strangle the man during his trial for murder. Even after Vanda was sentenced to 300-500 years in the state penitentiary, Bowers could not get over his anger and hatred:

"More and more my anger consumed me. My feelings about the loss of my sister and the man who took her life were so strong that sometimes I felt physically ill. Long after Margie's death, I continued to have moments when the tragedy felt unbearable and my anger unendurable."

Then one day, riding in his car, Bowers heard a man reading and talking about the Matthew 18, a passage in the Bible where Jesus tells his followers we should forgive others 70 x 7 times. Bowers, a follower of Jesus, was convicted. He says it was as if God spoke directly to him, saying, "When are you going to forgive?" Tom relates his reaction:

"Words that direct and powerful had never entered my mind before. The words had been so real it challenged what had been an underlying assumption in my life—I could never forgive Thomas Vanda. Yet I realized I had been making a choice not to forgive, a choice that was poisoning my life."

After much prayer and wrestling with God, Bowers made a conscious decision to follow Jesus in even this. When he was finally able to speak the words, "Thomas Vanda, I forgive you," as he describes, "A crushing burden was lifted from me, and I was filled with a transcendent peace."[70]

Thornton Wilder's play, *Our Town,* tells the story of people living in the fictional town of Grover's Corner, New Hampshire. The action takes place in the early 1900s, but the most interesting aspect of this play is the set. There isn't one. The entire play revolves around the relationships of people. Wilder's point in eliminating the set is that he wants you to watch the people. He communicates a powerful message that the relationships are what the play is about and what life itself is about.

Learning From God

Each of us in our lives also has a role in a play. We live our lives on a set—our jobs, our home, our car, and our recreational activities—but what our lives are really about is relationships with people. The circumstances are just the set of the play. It is our relationships to people which produce the drama, passion, and action in our lives. That is why the Bible is so important.

The Bible is a book about relationships. It is God's manual to help us learn how to guide and build our relationships so we can experience the abundant life he intends for each of us. The Bible is full of poetry, history, biography, and letters between friends. When we read the Bible, we learn a lot about God, but we also learn a lot about ourselves. He teaches us how we are made, what makes us happy and healthy, and what makes us miserable. He teaches us how to build strong loving relationships and how to repair them when they get broken. The Bible is one of the greatest spiritual resources God has given us. It can be yours by simply reading and learning from it on a regular basis.

Before you try to read the Bible, let me make a couple of suggestions. According to George Gallup's research, almost 90 percent of American households have at least one Bible. That's good. Unfortunately, about half of them are the *King James Version*. This is an English translation developed in 1611 as a "modern" alternative to the Latin text. At the time, it was contemporary and relevant. Of course, that was nine years before the Pilgrims landed at Plymouth in the New World! Like other aspects of the culture of this period, the *King James Version* is fairly difficult for most Americans to read and comprehend. I would suggest you avoid this translation of the Bible if you are a new believer.

God really wants to speak to you through his Word! So please get a Bible which is easy to read and understand. For new Bible readers, I suggest the *Good News Bible* (Today's English Version). *The Journey* is a Bible designed especially for people just beginning to explore God. It has a lot of helps for new readers. The New International Version is also good. I like *The Message,* which is a contemporary version of the New Testament. It's great for reading, but it lacks verse numbers, so it is a little harder to use for study or reference.

Don't bother getting an expensive leather Bible. A paperback will be fine to get started. Later, if you find a version that really works for you, then you can get a better quality Bible.

Avoid Bibles with a lot of commentary and remarks from some other author, such as the *Thomas Chain Reference Bible.* To learn about God, you need to read his Word and ask his Holy Spirit to teach you what it means for your life. Don't spend your time listening to a lot of other people trying to tell you what a passage means. That kind of study tool may be helpful after you've had more experience with God and his Word. But at the beginning, it can distract you from hearing God's voice through Scripture.

Getting started is not as hard as you might think. A lot of people take one look at the Bible and say, "Whoa! That's too big, too long, too complex! It's like *War and Peace* and then some! I couldn't possibly read that!"

It *is* possible. I'll try to give you a strategy for reading the Bible that is very manageable. Reading the Bible is easy; it's like eating an elephant. How do you eat an elephant? One bite at a time! The same is true for the Bible. If I showed you all of the food you would need to sustain you for the rest of your life stacked up in barrels and crates, you might also be overwhelmed. 160,000 pounds of raw food (it's like a pile of eighty Volkswagen Beetles) might make you want to gag and stop eating. But look at it one meal at a time, one day at a time, and it's not so overwhelming.

The same is true for the Bible. God has packed enough spiritual nutrition into the Bible to feed you, your family, and your friends for a whole lifetime. Don't think you need to eat it all in one sitting! You learn from the Bible one bite at a time.

Learning From God

When you read Scripture, you want to read enough of a passage to get its context and understand what is going on, but you don't want to read more than you can digest in a sitting. Each time you read God's Word, you want to take away a bit of comfort, a bit of learning, an insight or application you can take and use in your life for that day. Don't be a hog and try and read too much, or it will give you a spiritual tummy ache and you will have trouble learning.

For first time readers, I suggest you start with the Gospel of John, which is in the New Testament (the second half of the Bible). I recommend you read a little bit in sequence each day until you finish the story John is telling you about Jesus. Then I'd suggest you read the book of Acts (which follows the Gospel of John). This is the history of the early followers of Jesus. Then go back and read the other three Gospels (Matthew, Mark, and Luke), which will teach you even more about Jesus.

After you have spent some time reading the New Testament, I would suggest you dip into the Psalms and Proverbs which are in the middle of the Old Testament (the first half of your Bible). Then come back and read the letters that make up the balance of the New Testament: 1 Corinthians all the way through to the book of Revelations.

Before you sit down to read the Bible, stop and pray. Ask God to illuminate his words so you can understand them and ask him to give you an application you can take and use in your life for that day. Begin by asking him to speak to you through his Word.

When you read a passage of Scripture, read a large enough portion to get a sense of what is happening. Most modern translations break up sections and put little headers on them so you know what is happening. The second chapter of the Gospel of John for example, is broken into three stories or passages. The first is about what Jesus did at a friend's wedding. The second concerns a trip he took to the Temple in Jerusalem. The last segment (only three verses long) concerns Jesus' insights about human nature—a result of his trip to the Temple. After you read a section, ask yourself some questions about what you are reading: *What does it say? What is going on? How are the people relating to God? How are they relating to each other? Is there is a spiritual principle I learn from this passage? How could that principle apply to my life? What should I do about it, Lord?*

Bakht Singh was a Sikh born into a wealthy Indian family in the north of India. As a young man, he went to England to study agricultural engineering and then to Canada to gain practical experience in his field. In Winnipeg, Manitoba, he stayed at a YMCA where he met a young man who introduced him to the Bible. So hungry was Bakht to learn the truth of God, he sat up all night reading through the Gospels of Matthew, Mark, Luke, and John. At first he thought this was a Holy Book for Westerners only, until he read in John 1:29, "Look, the Lamb of God, who takes away the sin of the world!" The sin of the *world,* not the sin of the west! Suddenly, Bakht Singh knew this included him as well.

Then he read in John 3:16-17, "For God so loved the world [not just the west] that he gave his one and only Son, that whoever believes in him shall not perish but have eternal life. For God did not send his Son into the world to condemn the world, but to save the world through him." He had never heard that before! Since he had just read what Jesus had said to Nicodemus about being "born again," Bakht Singh knelt down beside his bed and asked the Lord to forgive his sins and to give him a new life. And Jesus did. From that moment on, Bakht Singh's life was changed.[71]

The Bible can be a powerful force for good in your life. If you will take time to read it regularly, it will reveal new truths, new insights, provide wisdom and guidance, and draw you into the mysteries of God's love. It is the best handbook you will have to learn who you are, what makes you tick, and how God has created you a unique and special person with great potential in life. You will learn about God's love for you and how Jesus can be your friend on a daily basis. You will discover the comfort, power, and encouragement of the Holy Spirit, who God sends into your life to live inside you and connect you to all of the resources of his love and power.

Drink deeply of the Bible. Take time to ponder it and learn from it on a daily basis. As you do, you will discover a verdant garden of spiritual fruitfulness and fulfillment springing up all around you and encouraging all aspects of your life.

Chapter Eighteen

NO LONGER ALONE

Reggie Morgan, who we met in Chapter 4 and Chapter 7, launched his new life with the help of a small group of friends. His sister Karen had known Jesus for years. In the past year, her adult daughter, her oldest son and his fiancé, and her husband Rick had all started walking with Jesus. Two classmates from high school, Dennis and Eileen McNamara completed this small circle of believing friends. Reggie finally made his decision to trust Jesus and try him out because of this small group. He gives this account of his experience: "As I wrestled with what to do about Jesus, I really felt this overarching sense of darkness, depression, and despair about my life. Finally, I asked my friends if they would pray for me. It was the first time I could ever remember asking for help. It was huge! The response was incredible. They just loved me, accepted me, and let me have room to work it out."

When Reggie took his first tentative steps of faith, he said, "All of a sudden I was overwhelmed with two feelings. I was engulfed in a profound sense of peace. And I realized I was no longer alone. It was the first time I felt safe, loved, and accepted in my entire adult life."

After learning to talk to and listen to God, discovering the process of learning from God's Word, the most important thing you can do for your own spiritual growth and health is to get involved in a community of believers. For a plant to grow and thrive and produce fruit, it needs to be in a good environment for growth. It needs deep rich soil that has good levels of nutrients. It must have adequate sun and rain if it is to grow. And it needs constant attention so the weeds don't grow to rob the plant of the vital nutrients it needs to be fruitful.

Your spiritual life is no different. You need to be planted in a group of friends who know and love Jesus and who can help you to grow. Community and your commitment to community are major factors, which will determine the health and vitality of your spiritual life and what it will look like in the long-term.

Dr. Gary Smalley, a well-known family counselor, offers some profound insights as to why community is so important for spiritual growth. He says all people need to be told by their parents that they are loved. Even if our parents cannot say it, or if they are dead, we still have this developmental need to be told we are loved. Smalley says we live in a time where there has been a massive generational failure to provide this love to kids. There are a variety of reasons for failure, but the damage is the same. We will treat our kids the same way we were treated unless the cycle is broken. Smalley says,

> The most effective way to help people change is through a small group. I've tried and seen lots of other ways to help adults change, but small groups are still the most powerful tool to help people change.[72]

A healthy small group of others who are friends of Jesus can actually re-parent us. It is a safe place where people don't induce blame or shame. There is the freedom to talk, to feel, to get connected to others so we can know we are loved.

As believers, we all have a need for family. When we begin to walk with Jesus and we put our faith in him, we are automatically adopted into God's "forever family." This is true on a spiritual basis, but it also needs to become true in our day-to-day lives. We each need a group to belong to, where God's family becomes a small band of people who know and love each other on a heart-to-heart basis. This small community of friends is where each of us can be known, where we can share intimately with others, and where we can receive support in times of suffering and hardship.

Are you part of a such a group? The test question I often ask people is: "How many 2 A.M. friends do you have?" Do you have people you would feel free to call in the middle of the night to help you out of a jam? When I lived in New Jersey, one of my 2 A.M. friends woke up in the middle of the night with appendicitis. I can't tell you how honored I was to have Dave call me in the middle of the night and ask me to come to his house and stay with his young kids so his wife Ruthie could drive him to the hospital. That's a real test of friendship.

When Martie and I lived in Illinois, we broke down on the tollway one night in 20-degree-below-zero weather, and in winds blowing 20 miles per hour. We had our twenty-month-old daughter with us, and Martie was eight months pregnant. Our car actually broke down twice and we were stranded at a rest stop in the middle of the prairie in the sub-arctic cold. At 5 A.M., we called our friend Terry who got a sitter for her four kids and then hopped in her station wagon and drove an hour and a half to rescue us. That is true friendship.

Do you have 2 A.M. friends in your life? You need to be part of a small group of believers who can develop the level of trust and support you need so you can call on each other in times of crisis.

The psychology of the dysfunctional family says there are three basic rules in dysfunctional families. No matter what the dysfunction—alcoholism, drug addiction, abandonment, emotional problems, sexual or physical abuse—the operating rules of the family are the same: *don't talk, don't feel, don't trust.*

Many of us have grown up in such homes. I know I did. Without God's help and the help of a small group to re-parent us, we are likely to impart these dysfunctional behaviors into our own relationships or families.

God wants each of us to be part of a new family of Jesus' friends. These friends help teach us how to talk, how to feel, and how to trust, so we can give and receive love from others the way God wants us to.

How can we learn a new way of relating to others? By the power of example! I remember a "Candid Camera" skit from the 1960s TV show. In this skit, the show rents a doctor's office for a couple hours. It sets up the hidden camera and has three fake patients (actors) come into the waiting room. The fake patients (a woman and two men) strip down to their underwear, fold up their outer clothes in a neat pile on their laps, and proceed to read a magazine. When real patients start to come in, they see three patients sitting in their underwear calmly reading. The camera captures the real patients' looks of dismay and careful observation of what the others are doing. After an interval, they too, strip down to their underwear and sit with their clothes folded, waiting for their turn to see the doctor. Each successive (real) patient does the very same thing. Can you believe the power of example?

When we are part of a small group that's loving, caring, and that reaches out in concrete ways to help others learn to walk in God's grace, we are part of a group that will have a profound and powerful influence for good in our lives. Left on our own, surrounded by a negative, critical, even hostile world, our spiritual life can get hammered. On our own and all alone, it is easy to get worn down and to lose our interest and motivation. Our spiritual health and vitality is sapped and drained because we are not in an environment which promotes healthy growth and fruitfulness in our lives.

Mike Doyle grew up in a town outside of Pittsburgh, Pennsylvania. Swissville was a steel town. Mike was raised in an Irish/Italian Catholic family and attended a Catholic grade school. He says of the Sisters of Charity, "They were the toughest females I ever met in my life, and I was scared to death of them! Back then I wasn't a real enthusiastic Catholic. I did it because I would have gotten beaten if I didn't do it. When I left for Penn State, I promised myself I'd never step inside a church again."

When Doyle was thirty-nine, he was elected to Congress. As a freshman congressman, Doyle was enfolded by a small group of new congressmen who met in Zack Wamp's office each week. Zack, a freshman congressman from Tennessee, invited Mike and a handful of others to the meeting. Each week they talked about themselves, their families, and shared interests in Washington. They concluded the session by praying out loud for each other. Doyle said this really freaked him out, "It was scary for me because I had never prayed in public." After weeks of meeting, the level of trust built in the group to the point where Doyle realized God was working in his life. It was like he was having a spiritual heart transplant. Finally, he was able to pray out loud in the group. "It was the beginning of a new experience for me with my faith and it changed my life. It absolutely changed my life. I'm happy to tell you those same six people who got together six years ago still continue to meet every Tuesday. It has changed all of our lives!"

Doyle shared about one of the impacts this small group had in his life. He tells how the group eventually taught him to say, "I love you." This radically changed his relationship with his second son, David. At the age of twenty, his son had completely tuned out his parents. He wasn't just rebellious; he was completely indifferent to them. Doyle says they felt like this son had completely shut them out of his life—that is, until the night Mike went home and sat his son down and said, "David, I love you."

"I hugged him and he started to cry. I realized it had taken me twenty years to figure that out." Almost immediately the relationship thawed, warmed, and began a healing process that is still continuing today. Congressman Doyle credits his small group with helping him identify the problem, realize the solution, and to have the courage to take the steps of change which rescued and healed his relationship with his son.[73]

I cannot overemphasize the importance of your involvement in a small group of like-minded believers to really grow in your new spiritual life. Jesus told his followers,

> "My command is this: Love each other as I have loved you. Greater love has no one than this, that he lay down his life for his friends" (John 15:12-13).

He went on and prayed for his disciples, saying,

> "My prayer is not for them alone. I pray also for those who will believe in me through their message, that all of them may be one, Father, just as you are in me and I am in you. May they also be in us so that the world may believe that you have sent me" (John 17:20-21).

Let me open a window on several small groups I am a part of. It will give you a taste of what group life is like. It's pretty simple, though there is a great deal of variation. Small groups are like faces. They have common features: eyes, noses, mouths, lips, ears—but each one looks different. My wife Martie and I are involved in three groups. We are in a couples group. One of the couples has been with us for seven years. Other couples have joined the group and left for various reasons over the years. Right now it's three couples—one in their early thirties, one in their early forties, and one who are close to their fifties.

We meet together every other week for an hour and a half to two hours. We talk about our marriages, our kids, our jobs, our parents, and whatever else is important to us. We laugh, we cry, we encourage, and occasionally we challenge each other. Sometimes we go out to dinner or go on a boat ride or a barbeque instead of having our regular meeting. We always talk about our spiritual lives, and often we will study a passage of Scripture or a book about spiritual issues. We share our needs, hurts, and hopes; and then we pray for each other. We try to stay in touch by phone or in person between meetings, and we try to pray regularly for each other as well.

Rick and George get together and play guitar or bike ride. Rick loves to take my family for rides in his ski boat in the summer. I always bring my hunting trophies and stories over to entertain Rick and Jen's three young boys. Often we will plan something we can do together and invite other friends who are spiritual seekers or just special friends in some way.

Martie, my wife, is involved with a women's group. This group grew out of her job at a local elementary school. A number of years ago, a first grade boy was hit and killed by a car while crossing a highway. My wife and a couple other teachers spontaneously gathered before school to pray for the grieving family, the kids at school, and others in the community affected by the tragedy. Other women on the school staff heard about the prayer meeting and asked to be included next time it happened. Now there is a group of twelve to fifteen teachers and staff, all women, who meet every Friday evening after school at one of the participants' homes.

In their meetings they share about their lives and concerns over tea and cookies, they do a Bible study from some kind of self-study material, and they pray for each other and their concerns. Occasionally they will go off and do something fun and social together.

One year, a bunch of them went to New York City for three days to see Broadway plays, museums, and to just have fun. From time to time, they will spend a whole meeting focused on one person who is in crisis, or on someone who needs to be listened to, cried with, encouraged, and prayed for. Some ladies have a strong faith experience. Others have none but want to explore and learn more about spiritual issues. It is a safe environment for people at all stages. Over the past six years, about a dozen women have found a personal relationship with Jesus by participating in this group.

I am part of a small group of men which we have fondly nicknamed "The Young Turks," a bit of a euphemism as the ages in the group have ranged from twenty-two to forty-eight. This group of men has been meeting together weekly for many years. We are all working guys, so we meet early—usually at 6:30 or 7:00 A.M. before work. Our only commonalities are that we are men, and we want to grow spiritually. We have had carpenters, a college student, an outdoor educator, a psychiatric social worker, a builder, a cop, a management consultant, a racecar engine builder and several salesmen in the group.

We usually have only an hour to meet, so we have coffee, share what's happening in our lives, laugh, joke, and tease each other. We spend thirty minutes looking at a passage of Scripture and talking about what God is teaching us, or where we need to grow. Then we pray for each other and take off for work. From time to time, we will ditch the regular format and go to our favorite greasy spoon diner and have breakfast together. When the landlocked salmon hit in April or the smallmouth bass go crazy in May, we shift our meetings to the lake and catch fish while we catch up on each other's lives, encouraging each other and praying for one another.

In some mysterious way, God says he will use our loving relationships with other believers to help those who don't yet know him come to faith. The kinds of relationships we have with our small circle of friends of Jesus will either confirm and validate the truth of God's love for others in our world, or our bad relationships will deny his existence and his love. 1 John 4:20 asks, "How can you say you love God, whom you cannot see, if you don't love your brother who you can see?" John goes on to say,

> Dear friends, let us love one another, for love comes from God. Everyone who loves has been born of God and knows God. Whoever does not love does not know God, because God is love (1 John 4:7-8).

> This is how we know what love is: Jesus Christ laid down his life for us. And we ought to lay down our lives for our brothers. If anyone has material possessions and sees his brother in need but has no pity on him, how can the love of God be in him? Dear children, let us not love with words or tongue but with actions and in truth (1 John 3:16-18).

Leath Anderson, a pastor of a church in the suburbs in Minneapolis, shared this story recently:

> "A few weeks ago I was in line at a Wendy's fast food restaurant. A woman I did not know came up and introduced herself to me. She mentioned she was attending Wooddale Church [the church Anderson pastors]. 'Tell me how you came to the church,' he asked.
>
> "'Well, last year I went through a terrible divorce in Iowa. Out of the divorce I got some furniture, the car, and our son... that's all. I didn't know what to do or where to go, so my son and I just got in the car and started driving. We drove north and came to Minneapolis. We slept in the car because we had no money and nowhere else to go. One Sunday we decided to go to church. We came to Wooddale Church and the first people we met said, 'So where do you live?' She said, 'We live in my car.' The immediate response of this believing

couple was, 'Well, then you come home with us. You can live with us.'"

"That night she and her son went there and ended up living with this family for several months. Another believer rented a trailer and drove to Iowa to pick up her furniture and brought it back to Minneapolis where a third family stored it in their garage.

"Then the woman shared, 'People in the church helped me to find a job and an apartment. Not having any money, things got tight. I knew the second month I wasn't going to be able to pay the rent. I was afraid I would lose the apartment. I went to church the next Sunday morning. A woman walked up to me I'd never met before and said, 'My husband just got a bonus. We prayed about what to do with this money. God told us to give it to you.' The woman handed me an envelope with $1,500 cash in it.'"[74]

This is an amazing story, but not uncommon. When God moves through those who know and love him, miraculous things happen. God is at work through people who follow Jesus. He's reaching out and helping people each day. It's not a program. It's not a ministry. It is simply one person who knows Jesus reaching out to help another person in need. Through this process of everyday miracles, Jesus is teaching many about his love and the free gift of grace he offers. When you become part of a small group of Jesus' followers, you will see this everyday miracle for yourself. You'll see it happen to people around you, and you'll see it in your own life. Seek God in a group of like-minded friends, and you will be able to experience the miracle of his love on a daily basis.

Chapter Nineteen

A FUTURE AND A HOPE

Now that you have begun to explore your relationship with God, what should you expect to happen next? Walking through life with Jesus is an adventure that will constantly open up new horizons and new opportunities. In short, you should expect the unexpected. You should expect the miraculous! Your life will never be the same. Now that you have committed yourself to a relationship with Jesus, you will discover he is invading every aspect of your life.

Jesus is alive and active. The Resurrection is not just a historical event, it is much more. It means the risen Christ will be present in all aspects of your life and will bring new growth, health, and vitality in ways you cannot even imagine. He is constantly at work transforming both our world and our lives! In Jesus, we have a future and a hope!

The gift of new life Jesus gives us is not merely a gift from God. It is the gift of God himself. He willingly comes and lives with us and in us through his Holy Spirit so his love, peace, and power are made available to us twenty-four hours a day, seven days a week. Jesus said when we trust him we would receive power of the Holy Spirit. Not power as *a gift* from the Holy Spirit, but the power we receive *is* the Holy Spirit himself living in us, helping us, guiding us, giving us strength, encouragement, comfort, counsel, and his ever-abundant peace and love.

Before Jesus, even if the circumstances of your life were really good—like a glass of water 7/8ths full—often your life probably felt sort of empty. Now that Jesus has come into your life, he has made a commitment to you—for the rest of this life and for all eternity—that he will be living in you through the Holy Spirit and will be available to you at all times. Even if the circumstances of your life are difficult, you will find your glass feels full. In Jesus we have a future and a hope!

What you need to do now is to look for Jesus. He is risen from the dead and he is alive and at work in the world today. He is alive and at work in *your* world. He will move into your life and do wonderful things which will surprise and amaze you. He is also at work in the lives of people around you. Be open. Pray for God to show you the people around you who he is at work in. People Jesus wants to hook you up with. You may be surprised!

Chuck Colson, who we met in Chapters 4 and 10, made his first steps of commitment to Jesus alone in his car. During the next week, he and his wife were on vacation, and Colson solidified his relationship and began to grow with Jesus. But then he headed back to Washington and the unfolding Watergate scandal. He had no idea what to expect.

The first week back, he was visited by a man named Doug Coe, who was a friend of Tom Phillips, the business executive who introduced Colson to Jesus. He welcomed Chuck as a brother in the faith and Colson opened up. As Colson says,

> Soon I found myself in growing excitement relating the story of my experience in Tom's driveway and the follow-up intellectual quest at a Maine cabin hideaway. "And so, Doug, I've asked Christ into my life. Nothing held back."

It was the first time I had articulated my commitment aloud to another person and the words startled me with their strangeness. Coe's smile broadened and his eyes shone as he repeated the words, "That's so exciting, just tremendous..." Then Doug shifted ground. "You'll want to meet Senator Hughes. Harold is a tremendous Christian."

I laughed. "Harold Hughes will not want to meet me. From what I've heard, he considers me the Number 1 menace to America. He's anti-war, anti-Nixon, anti-Colson, and we couldn't be further apart politically."

"That doesn't matter now," Doug continued with unabated exuberance.

"You are telling me that because I have accepted Christ, Harold Hughes, just like that, wants to be a friend?" I shook my head in disbelief.

"Wait and see, Chuck. Wait and see. You will have brothers all over this city that you never knew anything about."

Then Doug suggested that we pray together at my desk. At first I was concerned what my law partners would think if one of them burst through the door. But Doug was so natural and relaxed that I relaxed too. He thanked the Lord for bringing us together in the bonds of fellowship, for letting us know his love. I stumbled and stammered through my prayer; it was the first time I had prayed aloud with anyone in my life.

Doug meant it when he said that I had unknown friends in the city. The next day under Secretary of State Curtis Tarr, whom Nixon had brought to Washington from the presidency of Lawrence University, a strong personality whom I admired greatly although I had met him only once called. "Anything I can do for you, Chuck, just call. I'm with you all the way. Just keep it in mind. You've got a friend here."

I was so taken back that I hardly knew how to answer. Some of my erstwhile colleagues in the Nixon administration, even men I had placed into their high positions, had grown more distant as the accusations increased. Men in politics always watch their associations carefully and Watergate's ugly stain was being spread on a lot of bystanders with a broad brush. Yet in the days that followed, men whom I hardly knew did not hesitate to ally themselves with me, each with the same message spoken in a dozen ways: "As brothers in Christ, we stand together." There was, I discovered to my astonishment, a veritable underground of Christ's men all through the government. [75]

Eventually, Doug Coe arranged a meeting between Colson and Senator Harold Hughes. Hughes and Colson met with Senator Al Quie, a former Democratic congressman from Texas, Graham Purcell, and their wives. As they met and talked, Harold Hughes said, "Chuck, they told me that you've had an encounter with Jesus Christ. Would you tell us about it?" Colson shared his experience and his journey of faith since the time he was in Tom Phillips' driveway. After sharing the whole story, he concluded, "As a new believer, I have everything to learn, I know that. I'm grateful for any help that you can give me."

> For a moment there was silence. Harold, whose face had been enigmatic while I talked, suddenly lifted both hands in the air and brought them down hard on his knees. "That's all I need to know. Chuck, you have accepted Jesus and he has forgiven you. I do the same. I love you now as my brother in Christ; I will stand with you, defend

you anywhere, and trust you with anything I have."

I was so overwhelmed, so astonished, in fact, that I could only utter a feeble, "Thank you." In all my life, no one had ever been so warm and loving to me outside of my family. And now it was coming from a man who loathed me for years and whom I had known for barely two hours.

The others also offered their support and counsel. "Politicians are wary of anyone who faces indictment, but Christians stand together," said Graham Purcell, a judge in Texas before his election to Congress. "That's right," chimed in Al Quie. "We'll be with you. Stand tall."[76]

Colson discovered during the long agonizing ordeal that led to his indictment that Jesus is true and can be relied upon. Colson found that not only God stood by him and supported him, but he brought many other friends of Jesus to comfort and uphold both Chuck and his family through the experience. In spite of the circumstances, which included serving time in a federal penitentiary, Colson found that Jesus is alive and active. In him, Colson had a future and a hope, no matter how dark and difficult his present circumstances were.

Jesus has people for you. Ask him to show you the people in your world who love him and who can be friends with you and help you as you grow on your spiritual journey.

You also need to look and see where Jesus is working to help and serve those who are hurting and suffering in this world. Jesus told his disciples this story about what it would be like when people were lining up to go to their destination in eternity:

> "When the Son of Man comes in his glory, and all the angels with him, he will sit on his throne in heavenly glory. All the nations will be gathered before him, and

he will separate the people one from another as a shepherd separates the sheep from the goats. He will put the sheep on his right and the goats on his left.

"Then the King will say to those on his right, 'Come, you who are blessed by my Father; take your inheritance, the kingdom prepared for you since the creation of the world. For I was hungry and you gave me something to eat, I was thirsty and you gave me something to drink, I was a stranger and you invited me in, I needed clothes and you clothed me, I was sick and you looked after me, I was in prison and you came to visit me.'

"Then the righteous will answer him, 'Lord, when did we see you hungry and feed you, or thirsty and give you something to drink? When did we see you a stranger and invite you in, or needing clothes and clothe you? When did we see you sick or in prison and go to visit you?'

"The King will reply, 'I tell you the truth, whatever you did for one of the least of these brothers of mine, you did for me.'

"Then he will say to those on his left, 'Depart from me, you who are cursed, into the eternal fire prepared for the devil and his angels. For I was hungry and you gave me nothing to eat, I was thirsty and you gave me nothing to drink, I was a stranger and you did not invite me in, I needed clothes and you did not clothe me, I was sick and in prison and you did not look after me.'

"They also will answer, 'Lord, when did we see you hungry or thirsty or a stranger or needing clothes or sick or in prison, and did not help you?'

"He will reply, 'I tell you the truth, whatever you did not do for one of the least of these, you did not do for me.'

> "Then they will go away to eternal punishment, but the righteous to eternal life" (Matthew 25:31-46).

Ask God to show you where you can find hurting people you can reach out to help and love in his name. Look around and see where the risen Jesus is at work, reaching out and helping others. When Chuck Colson began to ask this question, he had just finished serving his prison sentence in Allenwood Federal Penitentiary, a white-collar minimum-security prison. His heart was touched by the lost, lonely, broken men who had been in prison with him. He began to pray and ask God to help him find ways to reach out and minister to the needs of this group of people. God blessed his efforts to share Jesus and his love with prisoners. Eventually he led Colson to found the ministry organization, Prison Fellowship. After twenty-five years, this ministry reaches out to people in every prison in the U.S., to prisons overseas, and even to the prisoners' spouses and families in eighty-eight countries around the world.

When I first read Jesus' command to reach out and help "the least of these," my wife and I were living in a nice suburb of Chicago, Illinois. I couldn't figure out how we were supposed to find the "widows and orphans," let alone the naked, hungry, thirsty, or prisoners. Our community had zoning, which did a pretty good job of keeping the less fortunate well away and out of sight. But we began to pray anyway, asking God to show us someone who we could reach out and help.

A few days later, Martie got a call from the associate pastor of the church we were attending. He asked her if she would go visit a young woman in the hospital with her sick baby. Martie was not at all sure how you visit a person you don't know, let alone how to do it in the hospital when their child is very sick, but feeling this was an act of faith and obedience, she went.

There she met Nicole Romano and her daughter Judy. Nicole had met her husband Rick when they were in high school. They dated, and after graduation married. Their relationship went well, as long as Nicole was able to keep Rick company down at the Red Dog Saloon in Carpenter, Illinois several evenings per week.

When she got pregnant with Judy, however, her pregnancy got in the way of her social life. Always somewhat thin and undernourished, Nicole had a difficult pregnancy. When Judy was born and developed health problems, it put a lot of strain on Nicole and Rick's home life and marriage. By the time Judy reached six months of age, Rick had had all the responsibility and commitment he could take. He left Nicole and Judy and moved in with a seventeen-year-old girl he picked up at the Red Dog. As far as he was concerned, marriage and his family days were over.

That's when we met Nicole and Judy. We befriended them, took time to help them through Judy's recovery, a difficult divorce, and the financial fall-out from Rick's desertion. Over the years, we have become closer than friends. More like brothers and sisters in Jesus. Our girls have always thought of them as Aunt Nicole and Cousin Judy. At one point, they even lived with us for a while. Over a period of five years, God helped them get back on their feet again, and Nicole eventually remarried and moved into a more positive period of life with a strong marriage and a happy family life.

So look for where Jesus is at work and pitch in. See how you can help. I once heard a woman speak who started a ministry for the homeless in Minneapolis. She said,

> "To each of us who knows Jesus, so much has been given and much will be asked. If you see somebody that needs to be helped, help him or her. If you see something that needs to be changed, change it. If you see something that needs to be done, just do it. Be Jesus' hands, his heart,

his feet, and his mouth. Let them meet Jesus alive and active in our world today. Every day you live, be beacons shining with the love of Jesus.

"There was a man who died and he went to heaven. He was all upset with God. He said, 'God, I see all this homelessness and this abuse, this war, and nobody helping anyone, and people killing each other. Why didn't you do something about it? Why?' God said and he said it well, "I did, I sent you."[77]

You need to look for where Jesus is at work—helping those who are spiritually hungry and thirsty around you. Are there people in your life who are looking for spiritual answers just like you are? Are there people in your life who are interested in learning how they can explore a relationship with God without getting religious? Perhaps God is at work in someone's life and all he needs is for you to be their friend and to share how Jesus has made a difference in your life.

This book is dedicated to Stu and Mary, two good friends of mine. I met both through business associations, and over time we became friends. Both are people who are looking for answers and asking challenging questions about life. When I told them I was thinking of writing a book on the topic of exploring God without getting religious, they both opened up and shared their own experiences with me. Each has been looking for spiritual answers but have had little success going through church or religious channels. In a sense, you could say I wrote this book for Stu and Mary.

When I was finishing the last few chapters of the book (Chapters 16,17,18), I knew there was a final chapter, but I didn't know what was supposed to go in it. I wasn't worried because I knew God would tell me what to put in it. Finally, when it was time to write this final chapter, I still had no idea what it was going to be about. Nothing but a blank page.

A Future and a Hope

I woke up Friday morning and was praying in the shower before I took off for a business meeting with Stu. The Lord said, "Tell them that Jesus is risen and active. He is alive and at work in their world today. Tell them to look for Jesus and get involved with what he is doing."

I thought, *Cool!* and proceeded to develop some ideas for the chapter as I drove to my meeting with Stu.

I have known Stu for eight years. He is a talented guy, has a Masters degree from Harvard, has enjoyed several successful careers, and is now an innovative entrepreneur. In short, he's your basic Renaissance man *and* a nice guy! We became good friends several years into our business relationship. I watched him meet and marry his beautiful wife, Lynda. Later they had a daughter, Julianna, and settled down into a stable and successful adulthood. Over the years, Stu and I have had a variety of conversations about my relationship with God and his spiritual search.

On the morning that I was supposed to write this last chapter, Stu came in, sat down, and said, "I want to talk about faith. Your faith and my faith." He went on to share how he'd been thinking a lot about his life. "When I look at the facts, my life is really quite good. I have a job I enjoy. I make great money. I have a wonderful wife and family, a terrific home life. I live in a great area, and I have enough free time to get involved in things I really care about. The facts tell me the glass of my life is at least 7/8ths full. So why does it feel like it's half-empty?"

He went on to tell me that for the past several weeks he had been having trouble sleeping. At night he would lay awake and ponder this sense that, while everything was great, something significant was missing.

"I've concluded that what I'm missing in my life is a relationship with God. Last night, I finally just started talking to God and told him I wanted to connect with him and have a personal relationship. I'm not exactly sure how you do that, but I really have a feeling God will show me how. After I told God this, I felt at peace for the first time in several weeks. I just felt his presence and was able to go to sleep."

How's that for God at work in my world? What a thrilling experience this was for me! Stu and I had a great time sharing. I told him more of my personal experience of getting to know God through Jesus. He asked if he could read the draft manuscript of this book. When he finished, he came back and told me, "I'm in! I am convinced the answers to life are found through a personal relationship with God through Jesus. Now tell me how I can share this good news with my friends."

Jesus is alive and at work in your world! He is quietly invading the lives of people you know and changing them for all eternity! Look for him at work in your world each day. Ask him to pour out his blessings on you and the people in your world. He will!

Let me conclude by sharing a passage of Scripture which is a description of my own personal experience of looking for God and his finding me.

> I waited patiently for the Lord. He turned to me and heard my cry. He lifted me out of the pit of destruction, out of the sticky mud. He stood me on a rock and made my feet steady. He put a new song in my mouth, a song of praise to our God. Many people will see this and worship him, then they will trust the Lord (Psalm 40:1-3 NCV).

My hope and prayer for you is that this will become your experience. Trust him that as you look for him, he will find you!

For Further Reading

To learn more or explore further, I suggest you take a look at the following books:

Mere Christianity, C.S. Lewis, 1943, Macmillan Publishing.

The Case For Christ, Les Strobel, 1998, Zondervan.

Christianity For Skeptics, Steve Kumar, 2000, Hendrickson Publishing.

For readers with a Jewish background:

Betrayed!, Stan Telchin, 1981, Chosen Books.

Christianity Is Jewish, Edith Schaffer, 1975, Tyndale.

For readers from other faith backgrounds:

More To Be Desired Than Gold, J. Christy Wilson, 1992, Gordon–Conwell Theological Seminary, So. Hamilton, MA.

Notes

[1] *Writing Toward Home*, Georgia Heard, pp. 1-2

[2] *Finding God at Harvard*, Owen Gingerich, 1996, pp. 268-73

[3] *Born Again*, Chuck Colson, 1976, pp. 32,33

[4] *In Search of Authentic Faith*, Steve Rabey, 1990, p. 93

[5] *Death Of A Marriage*, Pat Conroy, 1978

[6] *Boston Globe*, Adapted from Brian C. Mooney, 01/28/01

[7] *USA Today*, Volume 19 No. 119, Steve Andrea, 2001

[8] *Time Magazine*, December 9, 2000

[9] *Ibid*

[10] *Boston Globe*, September 14, 2001

[11] *Born Again*, Chuck Colson, 1976, p. 91

[12] *Pensees*, Blaise Pascal, Volume 33, edited by RL Hutchins, 1952, p. 244

[13] Deuteronomy 4:29

[14] Matthew 7:7-8

[15] *Finding God at Harvard*, Armand Nicholi, Jr., 1996, p. 111

[16] "The Unchurched American Study," conducted by Bruno & Ridgeway Research Associates for the American Bible Society, May 1997

[17] *World Magazine*, Lynne Vincent, 11/11/00, pp. 18-20

[18] Matthew 23:3-4

[19] Matthew 23:13-14

[20] Matthew 23:27-28

[21] *Writing Towards Home*, Georgia Heard, p. 24

[22] *Boston Globe*, Arthur Smith, 1/21/01

Notes

[23] *The Wonder of Being*, by Charles Malik, an article in *Finding God at Harvard*, p. 345

[24] *Finding God at Harvard*, Armand Nicholi, Jr., 1996, p. 114

[25] *Finding God at Harvard*, Krister Sairsingh, 1996, p. 184

[26] *The Daily Telegraph* (London), Victoria Comke, 3/23/01

[27] Matthew 15:1-9

[28] John 10:10

[29] *Finding God at Harvard*, Armand Nicholi, 1996, pp. 116,117

[30] John 3:16, Luke 10:16, John 10:10, Matthew 11:28, John 11:25-26, John 8:31-32, John 12:44

[31] *Finding God at Harvard*, Malik, 1996, p. 342

[32] *Ibid*

[33] *Finding God at Harvard*, Malik, 1996, p. 344

[34] John 1:3-5

[35] *Boston Globe*, July 1991

[36] Ephesians 2:8-9

[37] 2 Chronicles 15:2

[38] Acts 15:11

[39] Hebrew, Isaiah 64:6

[40] *Born Again*, Chuck Colson, 1976, p. 92

[41] *Born Again*, Chuck Colson, 1976, p. 93

[42] 1 Peter 3:15

[43] Luke 6:43-44

[44] James 1:5

[45] *Finding God at Harvard*, Armand Nicholi, Jr., 1996, p. 115

[46] 1 Corinthians 13:4-8,13

[47] "Two Ways to Heaven" (a sermon), David Morgan, 4/13/87

[48] *Ibid*

[49] *Ibid*

[50] Romans 3:23

[51] "Two Ways to Heaven" (a sermon), David Morgan, 4/13/87

[52] *Finding God At Harvard*, Glenn Loury, 1996, p. 67

[53] John 14:6, Revelation 3:8, Revelation 22:1

[54] *Walking on Water: Reflections on Faith and Art*, Madeleine L'Engle, pp. 28-29

[55] *Ibid*

[56] *Betrayed*, Stan Telchin, 1981, p. 100

[57] *Finding God at Harvard*, by Evelyn Lewis Perera, 1996, pp. 48-54

[58] *People Magazine*, Twist of Fate, 3/26/01

[59] *A Stone for a Pillow*, Madeleine L'Engle

[60] *Walking on Water*, Madeleine L'Engle

[61] *Ibid*

[62] *Finding God at Harvard*, Brent Foster, 1996, p. 130

[63] *Finding God at Harvard*, Armand Nicholi, Jr., 1996, p. 114

[64] *Walking on Water*, Madeleine L'Engle

[65] *Finding God at Harvard*, Brent Foster, 1996, p. 130

[66] *A Stone for a Pillow*, Madeleine L'Engle

[67] *A Stone For A Pillow*, Madeleine L'Engle, p. 125

[68] *Mere Christianity*, C.S. Lewis

[69] *USA Today*, November 21, 2000

[70] *Guide Post*, January 1999, pp. 6-9

[71] *More to be Desired than Gold*, Christie Wilson, 1992, p. 45

[72] "Keys to Loving Relationships" (video series), Gary Smalley, 1994

Notes

[73] *National Prayer Breakfast*—Leadership Luncheon speech, 2/1/2001

[74] "Congress on Evangelism" (speech), Leith Anderson, 2/3/2001

[75] *Born Again*, Chuck Colson, 1996, p. 133

[76] *Ibid*

[77] *National Prayer Breakfast*—Leadership Luncheon speech, Mary Jo Copeland, 2/1/2001

Exploring God Without Getting Religious

Someone you know probably gave you this book or suggested you get a copy. If you have questions or concerns about the material in the book, please go back to the person who connected you to the book. I am sure they would welcome the chance to discuss your thoughts and feelings. Start a spiritual conversation. It may surprise you!

If you are finished with this book, please pass it on to someone you feel might enjoy exploring the spiritual issues it discusses. If you are already a believer, give it to a seeking friend. If you are a seeker and this book has been helpful, pass it on to someone else asking spiritual questions.

This book is not available through your regular bookstore.

Our goal in publishing *Exploring God* is to get it directly into the hands of secular people who are asking spiritual questions. Our hope is that people asking spiritual questions will pass it around their network of friends where it will do the most good. Spiritually speaking, we are all just beggars. When you find a source of spiritual food, you need to let others know how to find it as well.

If you enjoyed this book and would like to obtain additional copies, our Web site is: *Exploringgod.com*

You may also order direct with a credit card from our toll free order line: *866-216-5433*

Or, you can order by mail. Send $14.95 per book plus $3.95 for shipping and handling (check or money order payable to New Life Center) and mail to:

Exploring God Book Order
P.O. Box 712
Wolfeboro, NH 03894

Growing With God: Learning to Walk with Jesus

Available Fall 2003

This powerful new sequel to *Exploring God Without Getting Religious* will teach you how to grow in your relationship with Jesus. A must for new followers of Jesus, this book will walk through practical daily steps you can take to create a fertile growing environment for your spiritual life.

Like any new relationship, learning to grow in your relationship with Jesus takes practical information, common experiences, and new perspectives to see what God is actually doing in your life. *Growing With God* will help answer many of your questions as a new believer. It will give you helpful strategies to develop new spiritual disciplines, which will enable you to discover the richness of spiritual resources God has put at your fingertips.

This book will also help you discover the exciting new world of relationships Jesus can bring you. In this new community of friends of Jesus, you will find your spiritual health and vitality growing on a daily basis.

For more information, please see our Web site this fall:

Exploringgod.com

The New Life Center
16 Depot Street
P.O. Box 712
Wolfeboro, NH 03894

603-569-6330
603-569-8469 (fax)
newlife@worldpath.net